Heart of New Testament Doctrine

THE RESURRECTION
Volume I

Gary R. Habermas

college press
Joplin, Missouri

Copyright © 2000
Gary R. Habermas

All Scripture quotations, unless indicated, are taken from
THE HOLY BIBLE: NEW INTERNATIONAL VERSION®.
Copyright © 1973, 1978, 1984 by International Bible Society.
Used by permission of Zondervan Publishing House.
All rights reserved.

Cover design by Mark A. Cole

ISBN: 978-0-89900-845-5

CONTENTS

Series Introduction	5
Study Introduction	7
1 Focusing on the Resurrection	11
2 A Sign for Unbelievers	20
3 The Truthfulness of Jesus' Teachings	35
4 Salvation	50
5 Raised Like Jesus	66
6 A Foretaste of Heaven	87
7 The Center of New Testament Theology	107

2000 AND BEYOND
STUDIES FOR SMALL GROUPS

In pursuit of our stated goal, "Every Christian a Bible Student," College Press has, since 1995, been publishing a series of *Studies for Small Groups*. These have proved very popular, both for group and individual study on a variety of topics and Scripture texts. Although, with the year 2000, we have changed the outward appearance of these study booklets, our commitment is still to providing solid, thought-provoking studies that will make a life-changing difference in the reader.

Of course, although we call these studies "for small groups," they are equally suited for individual study. If you are simply reading the book for your own benefit, please do take the time to use the "Reflecting on . . ." questions to focus your own thoughts. In a small group study, the questions should not only be used as a review, to see if you remember what was actually said in that lesson by the writer, but to help spark discussion of the further *implications* of the lesson material. Nor should you consider the questions that are provided the only questions to be asked. Any study is only as good as the effort you put into it, and the group leader should have read the lesson through thoroughly before the class meets, as well as encouraging all other members of the group to do so if possible. If the leader has gone through the lesson in advance, he or she will probably have thought of other questions, some of which may never have even occurred to the writer or editors of the study. After all, what is important is not just the bare facts of the lesson, but how they intersect with your own path in the Christian walk.

Above all, do not feel you have to race through the lessons. Although the number of lessons is purposely kept small so that no one has to commit in advance to an endless period of time on the study, you should not cut off discussion of an important issue just to fit the whole of the lesson into one study session. Nor do you want to leave off the end of a lesson because you didn't get it all in during the allotted time. The greatest advantage of the small group setting is the flexibility you have, allowing you to carry over discussion to the next session. Take full advantage of this flexibility.

THE RESURRECTION: HEART OF NEW TESTAMENT DOCTRINE

I've heard all the comments and jokes before: "What! Another book on the resurrection? Don't you ever finish this topic? Can you write on other subjects?"

"What does the 'R.' stand for in your middle name—resurrection?"

Then there was the joke in a student skit at the first college where I taught: "One day I was walking down the sidewalk and I bumped into Robbie Habermas." (The speaker was referring to my son who at that time was just three years old.) "Trying to make a little conversation, I said, 'Nice day, isn't it, Robbie?'"

"But Robbie cut the conversation rather short," the student continued. "'What does that have to do with the resurrection?' he asked me. Then he kept right on walking."

Five years later, Robbie was in his Sunday School Class during the Easter season. "How do we know the resurrection really happened?" the teacher asked, presumably looking for an answer like the Bible tells us so. Since Robbie had just recently asked me the exact same question at home, his hand shot up.

"How do we know George Washington ever lived?" he asked.

After an initial confused look, the teacher got the point. "Oh," he retorted, "you're Habermas's son, aren't you?"

But the clincher was a comment actually made to me by one of my college students, a class joker who struggled in more theoretical classes. "Whenever I don't know what goes in one of the blanks on your exams, I put the word 'resurrection' and I know I will get at least one-half credit," he said with a big chuckle. I laughed, too.

For many years I have been chiefly occupied with more theoretical and critical aspects of the resurrection of Jesus. With few exceptions, my seven other books on this subject have been directed to evidential concerns. Yet, throughout my studies I have repeatedly said that we need to move on to other aspects that reveal the richness of the resurrection. It has just seemed that there was always another critic to respond to, or another skeptical hypothesis to answer. But now the time has come to concentrate on the application of resurrection truth to other areas. We need to see what else God has for us in this marvelous event.

This is a popular book; it does not employ any technical language or discussion. All Scripture references, whether highly evidenced or not, are given the same weight. The authors of the biblical books are treated in traditional terms. Neither is this an apologetics text. Rather, my central theme is that the resurrection is related to many of our most cherished New Testament doctrines. In each case, the rallying point surrounds the greatest event in history.

To further the quest for relevancy, each chapter contains both an "Application" and "Reflection" section for careful consideration of lessons that can be both learned and applied. "Suggested Reading" lists, composed of sources for a general readership, make suggestions for further study.

OUR TOPICS

Look at some of the studies on Jesus' resurrection. They seem chiefly to focus on two central areas: apologetics and the gospel message of salvation. So when Christians think of this topic, it would not be surprising if they also directed their thoughts to these two subjects. After all, both of these messages are frequently found in the New Testament. Many wonderful books and articles have correctly centered on the gospel itself, as well as on defending the faith. These twin topics have been thoroughly addressed in the literature.

As crucial as these areas are, this stance would miss many other aspects of the resurrection, which play a much larger and intricate part throughout the New Testament. I have often said that the resurrection is like a many-faceted diamond. Turn it one way and, like looking into the depths of the elegant gemstone, one finds the very center of the gospel proclamation. From another angle, it is our chief evidence for the truths of Christianity. Turn it other ways and it is connected to many other treasured doctrines. When the light hits from still other directions, it is connected to many everyday practices in the Christian life. This event truly does present many varying perspectives and believers need to cultivate the richness of each.

We begin with a discussion of the resurrection as the very center of the New Testament message. Then we look at this event as a sign for hardened, open-minded, and sympathetic unbelievers. After addressing the nature of both the gospel facts and faith, we look at the truthfulness of Jesus' teachings, especially what He said concerning Himself. Then we move on to other theological topics and the light that is shed on them by the resurrection event. For example, we also link this great event to the believer's resurrection, as well as to other future events. Appropriately, our last topic concerns the glimpse that we get of heaven, provided for believers through the lens of the resurrection.

A follow-up, companion volume is entitled *The Resurrection: Heart of the Christian Life*. It will move on to another large area and link this event to numerous dimensions of living the Christian life. There it will be our purpose to provide a practical look at many of those biblical areas that interface with the resurrection of Jesus, turning the diamond around in the direction of daily applications. Every chapter likewise includes sections for application, additional reading, and discussion. Experiencing actual change in the Christian's life through the practice of truth is the major goal.

These twin volumes are meant to be studied one after the other. But benefits can also be gained even if they are studied separately.

While the resurrection will always remain both one of the facts of the gospel and the chief evidence for Christianity, it is also possible to miss the forest for the trees. This event likewise signals many other aspects of the Christian faith, including numerous practical insights. It will be our purpose here to examine some of the theological connections with the hope that a more rounded view of the centrality of the resurrection may be formulated.

1
FOCUSING ON THE RESURRECTION

In this lesson:
- ▶ Centrality of the resurrection to Christianity
- ▶ Broad application of the resurrection to all aspects of Christianity
- ▶ Dangers of separating the resurrection from other basic teachings

When I was two years old, I had gotten sick and developed a temperature of 105 degrees. My brother Ron, a year younger than me, was also sick with a temperature of 104 degrees. Somewhat alarmed, my mother took us to the doctor's office.

After an examination, the physician replied, "Your boys have the flu. I've seen dozens of cases like this in the last few weeks. A few days from now, they'll both be fine. If I were you, I wouldn't be concerned."

Focusing on the Resurrection

As my mother would recall later, it was his last few words that had caught her attention. "Well, if they were *your* boys," she thought to herself, "*I* wouldn't be concerned."

Without wishing any ill on her physician's children, my mother had made a worthwhile point. Things that are of central importance to me may not be as important to someone else. But they can mean *everything* to me!

> Many Christians realize that the atoning death, burial, and resurrection of Jesus Christ stand at the very center of Christianity.

Many Christians realize that the atoning death, burial, and resurrection of Jesus Christ stand at the very center of Christianity. To trust in this Jesus brings salvation (1 Cor. 15:1-4). With regard to the resurrection, perhaps the most publicized aspect has been the apologetic perspective, since believers seem to understand, along with Paul, that "if Christ has not been raised, your faith is futile; you are still in your sins" (1 Cor. 15:17; cf. v. 14). Aspects like the importance of this event, its highly evidential nature, and its unique miraculous content have attracted Christians to the study of the resurrection through the centuries. Understandably, there have been many efforts since the earliest church to defend it against its accusers.

However, unless we move beyond the apologetic aspects, literally dozens of New Testament texts will be in danger of being understated or even ignored. In this book, my purpose will not be to argue for the historicity of the resurrection but to explore the many senses in which this event serves other functions. My underlying contention is that the bodily resurrection of Jesus is a literal event in time-space history and that, as such, it provides a basis for Christian truth.[1]

THE HEART OF THE NEW TESTAMENT

That the resurrection of Jesus is the central claim in Christianity is recognized across a broad theological spectrum. Both conservative and liberal scholars acknowledge this, as do many academicians in between these opposite perspectives. There can be little question that this event is so closely related to Christian history and theology in the New Testament, that faith would be jeopardized without this teaching. After all, we are addressing the fate of Jesus Christ, who said that believers would live because He was alive (John 14:19). Our eternal future is tied to His! The resurrection is that link.

Further, the resurrection is also of primary importance in practicing the Christian life. New Testament authors connect it with such diverse topics as transforming lives, evangelism, dealing with doubt, suffering, and grief, plus providing daily power to conquer sin, be totally committed, and conquer the fear of death. These are the topics for our second volume.

> Our eternal future is tied to His! The resurrection is that link.

The chief passage addressing the centrality of the resurrection is 1 Corinthians 15. In verses 12-19, Paul faces squarely the issue of what Christianity would be without this event. The apostle does not soften his words; he thinks that nothing distinctive would be left to salvage. After recording an early tradition that he received from others that contains early testimonies from those who actually saw the risen Jesus (vv. 3-8), Paul turns to the issue of significance.

For Paul, if Jesus did not rise from the dead, all the apostolic preaching is useless (v. 14) and Christians give false testimony about their faith (v. 15). Further, Jesus' death accomplished nothing, for no one's sins have ever been forgiven (v. 17). If this were not enough, Paul continues with the even more painful comment that Christian loved ones who have died are lost; we will never be reunited with them again (v. 18). In short, Paul explains that, without Jesus' resurrection, Christians are more pitiable than all other people because they only possess hope in this world (v. 19). As Paul states twice in this passage, the Christian faith is futile if Jesus has not been raised (vv. 14,17).[2] We have no distinctly Christian hope.

> The truth or falsity of Christianity depends on the resurrection.

However, Paul changes the entire picture in the next verse. He corrects the dismal portrait he has just painted by asserting that Jesus has, in fact, been raised from the dead! So He is now the Example of the believer's resurrection, as well (v. 20). Paul is clear that the truth or falsity of Christianity depends on the resurrection.

While this chapter is often employed in an apologetic context, it should be noted that Paul turns just as quickly to some practical applications of the resurrection message. In verse 32, he appears to base Christian ethical concerns on this event, too. Without Christ's or the believer's resurrection, he says that we may as well enjoy all the good things in life, for we have no eternal future: "Let us eat and drink, for tomorrow we die." In other words, practicing moral living (including behaving for the sake of eternity) is otherwise groundless.

Then Paul turns to the question of the believer's resurrection body in verses 35–50. What kind of body will we have? How will we have ultimate victory over death? Like verse 20, all of this is viewed as a corollary of Jesus' being raised.

Focusing on the Resurrection

Then Paul ends the discussion with a challenge that we are therefore to both stand firm in faith and to commit ourselves to the Lord's work. The motivation for all of this is the double truth that Jesus was raised and that believers will be raised, too. Our labor for the Lord is not in vain (v. 58). So Christianity is anything but vain, as would have been the result, as Paul had said earlier, if Jesus had not been raised from the dead. To the contrary, everything flows from the truth of Jesus' resurrection.

In 58 wonderful verses, then, Paul moves through a range of topics (apologetics, theology, ethics, and practice), all resulting from the truth of Jesus' resurrection. He discusses the content of the gospel message (vv. 1-5) and the factual basis for Jesus' resurrection appearances (vv. 3-11), before moving to the importance of the resurrection (vv. 12-19), the believer's resurrection body (vv. 20-49) and immortality (vv. 50-57), and on to our commitment to God (v. 58).

> There is much more to the subject of the resurrection of Jesus than apologetics alone.

There are implications here for various subjects of vital interest to believers. As we have said, there is much more to the subject of the resurrection of Jesus than apologetics alone. The New Testament as a whole similarly relates a vast number of topics to this event, many of which seem seldom to be explored in much detail. In this book we will pursue a number of these themes and their connection to the resurrection.

A few examples might be helpful. Jesus and Paul use the resurrection as a sign for unbelievers. For many Jews, as well as for the early church in general, this occurrence indicated that God had approved of Jesus' message. The resurrection could not be separated from the content of the gospel, since it was intricately related to the message of the Kingdom of God, leading to conversion. As a result, the Christian church was born, with Sunday (resurrection day!) as the prescribed day of worship instead of the Jewish Sabbath. Lives were transformed, not the least of which was that of Saul of Tarsus, the persecutor of the church, who also met the risen Jesus. The resurrection also points to the Lord's return, is an example of the believer's resurrection body, and provides us with a foretaste of heaven.[3]

Each of these subjects has Jesus' resurrection as a chief ingredient. In many cases, it is the focal point. It is our purpose to examine each issue and attempt to ascertain the meaning for the early church, as well as an application for Christians today.

A CAUTION

A brief caution needs to be sounded before we continue to our first topic. It is not our purpose to separate the resurrection from Jesus' atoning death and burial, or from any other New Testament subject. To do such would be to do violence to the facts of the gospel by presenting them in a disjointed, piecemeal manner. Jesus' death was a prerequisite for His resurrection, while the former without the latter would have no forgiving power, as Paul himself argued (1 Cor. 15:17).

> Jesus' death was a prerequisite for His resurrection, while the former without the latter would have no forgiving power.

So these facts form a single unit, and the New Testament speaks of them that way, too. To separate this grand event from other truths would be to do violence to both its nature and func-

Focusing on the Resurrection

tion. In this sense, then, the resurrection ought not be viewed as an isolated fact.

On the other hand, the New Testament frequently does speak of the resurrection as a unique event, perhaps to highlight its distinctive nature. However, this is still not to detach it from the overall Christian message. In particular, the cross and the empty tomb function together: the Jesus Christ who died is the same One who arose from the dead and appeared to many people (1 Cor. 15:3-8). Therefore, when the subject of the resurrection is in view, it should not be thought that it is being separated from the rest of the Christian gospel or theology.

APPLICATION

This chapter has introduced a broad theme—the centrality of the resurrection in the New Testament. From our very general overview, we may draw a couple of application points for today.

For too many of us, the resurrection is an isolated event. While it is the very center of the gospel message and the chief evidence for Christianity, it too frequently does not go any further

> For early Christians, the resurrection was a many-faceted event that paved the way for both theoretical and practical concerns.

than this. Yet, for early Christians, the resurrection was a many-faceted event that paved the way for both theoretical and practical concerns. It was not only *the* key to apologetics and theology as a whole, it also had much to say about the Christian life.

Similarly, believers today should view the resurrection as did the earliest Christians. While still recognizing its importance in

Resurrection: Heart of New Testament Doctrine

the areas of the gospel and apologetics, increasing attention ought to be paid to its value in theology as a whole. It also should be at the center of everyday issues involved in living for Christ. For example, it is one of the keys to applying the Christian disciplines — those practices that encourage and develop our walk with our Lord. It is clear that, for the New Testament writers, to miss these points is to neglect a crucial ingredient.

NOTES

1. The author has written seven other volumes on the historicity of the resurrection that may be consulted by the reader who is interested in this aspect. For a couple of examples, see Gary R. Habermas, *The Historical Jesus: Ancient Evidence for the Life of Christ* (Joplin, MO: College Press, 1996). A more technical discussion of some of these issues can be found in Gary R. Habermas and Antony G.N. Flew, *Did Jesus Rise from the Dead? The Resurrection Debate*, edited by Terry L. Miethe (San Francisco: Harper and Row, 1987).

2. In 1 Cor. 15:14,17, Paul uses two different Greek words to express the futility of the Christian faith if Jesus has not been raised. The first term (*kenon*, v. 14) indicates a sense of emptiness while the second (*mataia*) emphasizes purposelessness or even the reporting of a falsehood.

3. These are some of the topics that are discussed in this book. Biblical references will be supplied in the appropriate chapters where each is discussed.

SUGGESTED READINGS

Green, Michael. *The Empty Cross of Jesus.* Downers Grove, IL: InterVarsity, 1984. Chapter 11.

Orr, James. *The Resurrection of Jesus.* Grand Rapids: Zondervan, 1908, reprint, 1965. Chapter X.

Tenney, Merrill C. *The Reality of the Resurrection.* New York: Harper and Row, 1963. Chapter IV.

Focusing on the Resurrection

Reflecting on Lesson One

1. Are evangelicals justified in speaking predominantly about the role that the resurrection plays in the gospel and apologetics, given their centrality and importance? Should other topics be treated with the same degree of attention, or given more of a subsidiary role? Why or why not? Support your answer.

2. Make a list of other areas — both theological and practical — that the New Testament relates to Jesus' resurrection. Provide references for each one. Can you anticipate some of the topics that we will consider?

3. Do you think that the analogy of the multifaceted diamond is a good one for explaining the many roles played by the resurrection? Can you give a better example? Why do you think another comparison would be preferable?

4. For group discussion: Do you think there is a need for the caution given in this chapter? Are believers in much danger of separating the resurrection from the rest of the gospel facts, or from other aspects of New Testament teachings?

Consider this:

The resurrection is the most powerful evidence we have that Christianity is real, yet many walk away from hearing this story unconvinced. In preparation for lesson two, think about how you would explain this resistance by some people to the gospel message.

2

A SIGN FOR UNBELIEVERS

In this lesson:
- Biblical examples of hearers of the gospel message and their various reactions
- How Jesus responds to these reactions
- The responsibility of Christians to proclaim the message

I'd heard about him from a friend of mine. Sneering at the uselessness of religion, Chris was an engineer and a skeptic who would debate with Christians, telling them that they had absolutely no evidential basis for their faith. "Please try to talk to him," our mutual acquaintance asked me.

Chris and I arranged a luncheon soon afterwards, while I was on the west coast for a speaking engagement. While we sat

A Sign for Unbelievers

there, he fired a volley of questions at me. I addressed each one, being sure not to sound overconfident or cocky. Then I brought up some evidences for Christian theism. As always, the resurrection of Jesus was the centerpiece of my presentation.

We talked well past the lunch hour. Chris indicated that he needed to do some thinking about everything he had just heard. Soon afterwards, he became a Christian. Speaking to him years later, he told me that our visit not only led to his conversion, but he had afterwards become an active member of a growing church. He also had become interested in apologetics. Several times since, he had met with friends and relatives, but now he had changed roles — he was doing the witnessing!

> If the resurrection is such a powerful evidence, why doesn't everyone who hears the message become a Christian?

This story raises another question. If the resurrection is such a powerful evidence, why doesn't everyone who hears the message become a Christian? Why do some walk away without trusting Christ?

There are several instances in Scripture where hardened unbelievers are confronted with outstanding signs of God's actions. In the Old Testament there are examples like the Israelites crossing the Red Sea, or the confrontation between Elijah and the prophets of Baal. In each case, there must have been a few nervous moments when believers stood against their unbelieving counterparts before the final outcome. What if God didn't act? But then everyone witnessed the awesome outpouring of divine power. God had acted.

The New Testament counterpart to these miracles is the resurrection of Jesus. On numerous occasions it was proclaimed as the chief indication that Jesus really was who He said He was, an event that even skeptics couldn't refute. They could evaluate the evidence for themselves. So how did they respond? That depends . . . .

FOR HARDENED UNBELIEVERS

On one occasion, Jesus was challenged by the scribes and Pharisees. Calling Him a teacher, they asked Him to produce a sign that would indicate the truthfulness of His teachings (Matt. 12:38-40). Jesus responded that those who require such miracles are wicked and adulterous, a frequent biblical reference to the Jews' spiritual apostasy. Still, Jesus indicated that a sign would nevertheless be given, even to such skeptics. The case of Jonah would provide an illustration of Jesus' burial and resurrection three days later.

> Jesus indicated that a sign, the "Sign of Jonah," would be given even to skeptics.

A similar instance is reported in Matthew 16:1-4, where Jesus was again tested, this time by the Pharisees and Sadducees. They also requested a sign indicating His authority. On the surface, at least, this was a somewhat odd scene. These two groups of Jewish scholars represented a wide theological spectrum; the Pharisees were sometimes thought of as the theological "conservatives" while the Sadducees were viewed as the theological "liberals" of that time. But they agreed on a question for Jesus. After referring to their spiritual apostasy, Jesus repeated His earlier comment. The sign of Jonah — Jesus' resurrection — would be given to them. Then Jesus walked away from them.

A similar challenge occurred earlier in Jesus' ministry when He was in Jerusalem. The Jews asked for a sign that He had the

A Sign for Unbelievers

authority to disrupt the daily business at the temple (John 2:18-22). Jesus told them that if they destroyed this temple, He would raise it up again in three days. John explains that Jesus referred to His own death and resurrection, as the disciples recalled afterwards (vv. 21-22). But the Jews misunderstood Him, thinking He was referring to the building in Jerusalem.

In these discussions, we find a very interesting contrast. Jesus predicted the sign of His resurrection even when He knew that His hearers would not believe in Him, regardless of what happened. John tells his readers that Jesus was well aware of his hearer's unbelief in spite of the miracles that He performed (John 2:23-25).

> Jesus predicted the sign of His resurrection even when He knew that His hearers would not believe in Him, regardless of what happened.

In both of Matthew's accounts, we find similar situations. Jesus recognized the spiritual apostasy of His questioners. Members of these groups had heard Him speak on several occasions and had witnessed other miracles, yet there was apparently no affect. Their lack of spirituality had been revealed by their own words, too. In the first instance, Jesus concluded that those of Jonah's day would condemn this generation for not believing even after personally hearing Him (Matt. 12:31). After the second episode, Jesus walked away (Matt. 16:4), apparently concluding that nothing was to be gained by continuing the discussion. This is reminiscent of John's comment that He knew men's hearts.

Another account with a similar message is the story of the rich man and Lazarus, found in Luke 16:19-31. Here it is the rich man who is hardened, enjoying his lavish living conditions while

24 A Sign for Unbelievers

repeatedly ignoring poor Lazarus's plight as he sat in front of his gate. Both men died, and Lazarus experienced a blessed existence. But the rich man asked permission from Abraham to return in order to warn his five brothers of the horrible torment that he experienced after death. Abraham denied his request, stating that if the brothers would not hear Moses and the other prophets, neither would they repent even if the rich man returned to them from the dead.

This story raises the intriguing question of whether Jesus had a further meaning in mind —that if the Jews were not convinced by the Old Testament Scripture, neither would they believe Him even after His own resurrection from the dead. Many Jews, in fact, did not turn to Christ's teachings even after that event.

Yet, we also know that many Jews did trust Christ, largely because of the resurrection. Some of these could be fairly described as hardened, too. What about Saul of Tarsus, the persecutor of Christians, who stood by and watched Stephen die a slow, horrible death by stoning? And there is James, the brother of Jesus, who scoffed when his brother came to preach. Here were two skeptics who hated the Christian message with a vengeance. Both were also completely changed by witnessing an appearance of the risen Jesus. We'll return to these situations later. For now, we will just conclude that Jesus' statements about the Jews were not exclusive, but were general comments aimed at describing the majority response.

> God does not force anyone to love Him.

There is certainly another important message here, as well. God does not force anyone to love Him. There is also a crucially important volitional aspect to faith: if an individual wills not to respond to Christ, he is not forced to do so. Further, even the awe-inspiring event of Jesus' resurrection will not compel anyone to believe against his or her own will. Sometimes people are so settled in their private beliefs that even such a miracle would make no ultimate difference!

Then why did Jesus mention His resurrection to such individuals at all? In what sense was it the ultimate sign? There are several possible responses, each of which provides part of the answer. Initially, Jesus' resurrection was not just performed for those who were spiritually hardened. It was meaningful for many others who witnessed His appearances or heard about them later, even if everyone was not convinced. Further, some skeptics such as Paul and James, the brother of Jesus, were still converted by appearances of the risen Jesus. Lastly, perhaps the people of Jonah's and Solomon's time will witness against the Jews who rejected Jesus (Matt. 12:41-42) precisely for the purpose of leaving them without an excuse — they could not claim that they did not receive a fair chance.

FOR OPEN-MINDED UNBELIEVERS

The resurrection of Jesus not only served as a sign for the spiritually apostate, whether or not they believed. It was much more frequently employed as the center of the Christian proclamation to unbelievers who were willing to hear the gospel. This scenario was very common in the Book of Acts, where on numerous occasions preachers like Peter and Paul presented the gospel message of the death and resurrection of Jesus Christ, with this great miracle functioning as the chief evidence. It is not our intent to discuss each of these instances here, but rather to concentrate on one passage that will serve as an example. In many of the instances where the resurrection was used in this manner, we

26 A Sign for Unbelievers

are told that a number of people became believers.[1] So it should not be denied that using the resurrection as evidence frequently resulted in salvation.

In Acts 17:16-34, while Paul was in Athens waiting for friends, he frequented both the local synagogue and the marketplace. In both locations he preached about Jesus and His resurrection before many Jews and Greeks, including Epicurean and Stoic philosophers, who later took him before their colleagues at a meeting of the Areopagus. As Paul addressed this group of thinkers, his initial point of contact was the many idols that he had seen in the city (vv. 16,22-23).

> Using the resurrection as evidence frequently resulted in salvation.

Paul presented at least four subjects during this lecture. He appears to have spent a good amount of time drawing parallels between the true God and some prominent Greek ideas, such as God's act of creation and His relationship to man. Apparently in an effort to find some common territory between them, Paul quoted a couple of the Greek scholars themselves (v. 28). But he also made it clear that these Greeks were still not worshiping the true God except through ignorance (vv. 22-29).

Moving to the need for salvation, the apostle explained that God required repentance of all people (v. 30), and He would also judge everyone accordingly (v. 31). Paul concluded that God had evidenced these truths by raising Jesus from the dead (v. 31).

Some members of Paul's audience sneered at his message, perhaps reminiscent of the hardened Jewish unbelievers who heard Jesus. Others, however, wished to hear more and even invited Paul to speak to them again (v. 32). A third response was one of faith; we are specifically told that a number of listeners became believers (vv. 33-34).[2] Especially remembering that some of these persons were philosophers (such as Dionysius, a member of the Areopagus), we get a sense of the appeal of Paul's message. The Holy Spirit was active that day. Here and elsewhere in the Book of Acts, salvation resulted when individuals responded positively to a message where the resurrection played an evidential role.

> Salvation resulted when individuals responded positively to a message where the resurrection played an evidential role.

FOR SYMPATHETIC UNBELIEVERS

Our final type of non-Christian is one who has heard the gospel message, perhaps even many times, but who has not responded in faith. There is every indication, however, that they are very interested. While fewer of this variety are singled out in the New Testament texts, Thomas may be one example (John 20:24-29).

A case could be made either way with regard to Thomas's salvation prior to having met the risen Lord. However, it seems likely that he was not a believer before that time, based on both his claim to disbelieve the literal resurrection of Jesus (vv. 24-25) and Jesus' statement that Thomas had believed *after* witnessing Him standing before him, alive (v. 29).[3]

At any rate, Thomas indicated to the other apostles that he had to see the resurrected Jesus for himself before he would believe. A week later his uncertainty was challenged by a face-to-face encounter with the Lord! Imagine Thomas's face! He could no longer deny the truth. He realized that Jesus was alive and worshiped Him as God (vv. 27-28). But it had taken a literal appearance of the resurrected Jesus to convince Thomas to believe. Jesus' own response is very instructive. Though he fulfilled Thomas's request, He also issued a mild rebuke: He preferred that Thomas had believed without needing sight (v. 29).

Another example where a sympathetic unbeliever is confronted with the truth of the resurrection is the case of Cornelius (Acts 10). When God sent Peter to testify to those who had gathered in his home, a portion of the sermon addressed Jesus' resurrection, reaching a crescendo in the salvation message (vv. 39-43). The result was that Cornelius and others received the message and the Holy Spirit (vv. 44-45). It appears that it was Peter's witness to Jesus' death and resurrection that led directly to the salvation of his hearers.

> It appears Peter's witness to Jesus' death and resurrection led directly to the salvation of Cornelius and the others.

APPLICATION

This subject presents several opportunities for interaction. Three points will be mentioned, providing useful topics for our reflection and action.

First, a most intriguing question concerns Jesus' apparent change of attitude toward those who asked for signs. With the Jewish leaders, Jesus was forceful, commenting on their spiritual adultery, and speaking of their judgment. With Thomas, only a mild rebuke was issued, explaining that he should have believed without asking for sight.

In yet another instance, although he was dealing with a

believer, Jesus' response was milder still. From prison, John the Baptist sent his disciples to ask whether Jesus was the Messiah, or should he be looking for another (Luke 7:18-28)? I think we underestimate the seeming seriousness of these last two questions. During an emotional time, John appears not to be sure of Jesus' identity. Jesus responded by performing miracles on the spot and then sent the report back to John (vv. 21-23). Although no rebuke was given, Jesus encouraged John the Baptist not to lose heart (Luke 7:23). But further, Jesus even gave John the ultimate compliment regarding his greatness, and precisely during the time of his doubts (Luke 7:28)!

What determined the different sorts of response on Jesus' part — from proclaiming judgment, to appearing to Thomas along with issuing a mild rebuke, to performing several miracles and giving a word of encouragement? In all likelihood, the differences in Jesus' replies were determined by the attitude of the individuals with whom He was speaking. The hardened hearts that refused to believe no matter what received the least gratification. The sympathetic heart and the believing heart were both met on their own terms, with the latter even being given a fantastic compliment. The point here may be that Jesus was not necessarily bothered by doubts or even by certain requests for evidence; the crucial issue appears to be the mind-set of the persons in question.

> The crucial issue appears to be the mind-set of the persons in question.

Second, what about the biblical statements that believers ought to live by faith rather than by sight, as in the case with Thomas?[4] But if this question is taken to imply that any visual evidence is a perversion of Christianity, then Jesus ought not have answered John the Baptist by doing miracles, or appeared to Thomas at all.

Then what did Jesus prefer that Thomas do instead of requiring sight? The most plausible answer is that Thomas should have believed that Jesus was raised from the dead based upon the testimony of the other disciples (see John 20:24-25). After all, without hearing the report of Jesus' appearances, Thomas wouldn't even know that they had occurred. Although this would not have been quite the same as seeing Jesus for himself, this would still be very strong evidence — the same sort reported in the New Testament and which believers accept today.

Interestingly enough, in each of the verses we just listed that require faith, the resurrection is also mentioned in the same context.[5] Perhaps the point here is that we *should* accept the testimonies of those who have seen the risen Jesus, otherwise, like Thomas, we wouldn't know the content of the gospel proclamation. But this is not the same as requiring that Jesus appear to us!

> Thomas's problem was in disregarding his colleagues' testimony and requiring personal sight.

If Thomas had believed the testimony of the other apostles, there could hardly have been an issue — all Christians today also believe by hearing and trusting the reports of Jesus' resurrection appearances. Thomas's problem, then, was in disregarding his colleagues' testimony and requiring personal sight.

But there is an additional point here, too. Jesus seemed to *prefer* that His hearers accept Him on the basis of His words, rather than for His miracles. But this does not mean that He did not recognize the validity of believing because of His miracles (cp. John 10:37-38 with John 14:11). Otherwise we would have a very difficult time explaining the New Testament emphasis on the evidential value of the resurrection, some of which we have seen in this chapter.

While Jesus and the New Testament authors do speak out against requiring *sight*, like Thomas did, they do not condemn having a proper attitude toward the evidence. John Stott says it well:

> But it is a great mistake to suppose that faith and reason are incompatible. Faith and sight are set in opposition to each other in Scripture (2 Cor. 5:7), but not faith and reason. On the contrary, true faith is essentially reasonable . . . . A believing Christian is one whose mind reflects and rests on these certitudes.[6]

A last lesson to be learned is that unbelievers can still come to know Christ in ways similar to those in New Testament times. A presentation of the resurrection of Jesus may still be a major motivating factor in the salva-

> The New Testament does not condemn having a proper attitude toward the evidence.

tion of people today, just as it was when Peter or Paul preached. We must acknowledge, of course, that saving faith is due to the work of the Holy Spirit and not to the persuasiveness of the Christian. Many personal testimonies have, in fact, pointed to the importance of the resurrection in the individual's decision.[7]

So even if it does not appear that people are coming to Christ in this manner, it is still crucially important to defend the faith anyway. As Francis Schaeffer has reminded us, if we do not help each generation to understand the truth of the historical Christian faith, it is difficult to expect that they will realize that there really are answers to their questions.[8] Who knows what effect such a presentation of the gospel might have later in those who have heard, even if they initially reject the message? So we must be faithful in proclaiming the death, burial, and resurrection of Jesus Christ today, just as Peter, Paul, and others did in the First Century. We should be faithful in this even if it appears that no one is listening to us.

The resurrection of Jesus was the major message for various sorts of unbelievers in New Testament times. Similarly, Christians today should not shy away from either answering questions or otherwise taking opportunities to explain the evidence for this event.

NOTES

1. For many of these examples, see Acts 2:22-24,29-33; 3:15,26; 4:2,10,33; 5:30-32; 10:39-43; 13:27-39; 17:1-4,18,31; 26:23. We will take a closer look at some of these texts in our follow-up volume, *The Resurrection: Heart of the Christian Life*.

2. This passage is helpful in illustrating our earlier point about the different ways people respond to the gospel message. It might even be said that the three divisions of people in this chapter are all represented among Paul's listeners. Those who sneered could well have been hardened unbelievers. Those who wanted to hear Paul again sound like open-minded unbelievers. Those who actually responded in faith were sympathetic unbelievers who became Christians.

3. We should note that even if Thomas was, in fact, a believer before meeting the risen Jesus, this discussion is still relevant, but would more properly be the subject of our discussion of Christian doubt in *The Resurrection: Heart of the Christian Life*.

4. Cf. John 20:29; Rom. 8:24-25; 2 Cor. 5:7; 1 Pet. 1:8-9, for examples.

5. Cp. John 20:19-23 and 20:29; Rom. 8:11 with 8:24–25; 2 Cor. 4:14 with 5:7; and 1 Pet. 1:3-5 with 1:8-9.

6. John R.W. Stott, *Your Mind Matters: The Place of the Mind in the Christian Life* (Downers Grove, IL: InterVarsity, 1972), p. 34.

7. For two examples, see Viggo B. Olsen, *The Agnostic Who Dared to*

Search (Chicago: Moody, 1974), especially pp. 34-47; Frank Morison, *Who Moved the Stone?* (London: Faber and Faber Limited, 1930, 1962), especially Chapter I.

8. Francis A. Schaeffer, *The God Who Is There: Speaking Historic Christianity into the Twentieth Century* (Downers Grove, IL: InterVarsity, 1968), pp. 139-140.

SUGGESTED READINGS

Ankerberg, John and John Weldon. *Do the Resurrection Accounts Conflict? And What Proof Is There That Jesus Rose from the Dead?* Chattanooga: Ankerberg Theological Research Institute, 1990. Pp. 154-165.

Ladd, George Eldon. *I Believe in the Resurrection of Jesus.* Grand Rapids: Eerdmans, 1975. Chapters 4–6.

McDowell, Josh. *The Resurrection Factor.* San Bernardino, CA: Here's Life, 1981. Chapter Eight.

Morison, Frank. *Who Moved the Stone?* London: Faber and Faber Limited, 1930, reprint 1962. Chapter I.

Olsen, Viggo B. *The Agnostic Who Dared to Search.* Chicago: Moody, 1974. Especially pp. 34-47.

Reflecting on Lesson Two

1. Why is it that studying miracles (or even experiencing them) does not always aim us in the right direction? What are some of the advantages and disadvantages of miracles serving as pointers to God?

2. What other biblical passages can you find that record unbelief even after a miracle occurred? Does Numbers 14:11 help to provide some direction? How about John 10:31-33,37-39? Do these texts shed some light on the rejection of Jesus by Jewish leaders in the passages we viewed?

A Sign for Unbelievers

3. Can you think of any hints in the Old Testament that the Messiah would be a miracle-worker or that He would be raised from the dead? What about Jesus' quotation of Isaiah in Luke 4:16-21? Could any of these passages have helped Jesus' Jewish listeners to understand Him better? Make a chart of some of the texts and jot down some of the directions you would pursue.

4. In light of the last question, can you guess what passages Paul might have used in his practice of visiting synagogues, using the Old Testament to show Jews that Jesus was the Messiah who died and rose from the dead (Acts 17:2-3)? Note that some came to the Lord by this method (v. 4).

5. Do you agree with the author about how to solve the question concerning faith, sight, and eyewitness testimony? State reasons for your position using relevant biblical texts.

6. How do you think believers today should use the resurrection in evangelism? How relevant is all the evidence we have for this event? Be sure to state your answer in terms of the biblical data rather than just giving your position.

Consider this:

In preparation for lesson three, determine your answer to the following applicable question. If you are a believer, what was it about Jesus or the gospel message that caused you to be willing to put your trust in Him? If you are not a believer, what would it take to convince you that Jesus was absolutely dependable and someone to whom you could trust your life?

3

THE TRUTHFULNESS OF JESUS' TEACHINGS

In this lesson:
- Why people feel the need for validation of the message
- Jesus' controversial claims
- The purpose of miracles as God's seal of approval

Have you ever considered making a purchase but a parent or friend told you not to do so until you first checked the warranty? Without such a guarantee, were you nervous? Conversely, upon being satisfied that the item carried a strong brand name, did you feel better about the deal? We've probably all had times when a nationally known "stamp of approval" was all we needed to make us feel comfortable. There's something about knowing that someone trustworthy will stand behind the product.

36 The Truthfulness of Jesus' Teachings

I think Christians often underestimate the mind-set of first-century Jews who heard Jesus speak. How would we respond if we discovered someone who really seemed to have the secret to life, but we couldn't find the sort of warranty that we wanted? After all, our most esteemed teachers not only told us that they didn't agree with Him, but they called Him a heretic. What if they warned us that we were placing our souls in eternal jeopardy? Would you feel very secure in your desire to trust His message of salvation? How could you know that He spoke the truth? Where is the divine stamp of approval that you would like so much to have?

Many listeners to Jesus' sermons concluded that He was Who He claimed to be, and they placed their trust in Him. Different credentials appealed to different people. Sometimes all they needed was to hear the authority with which He spoke that was so unlike that of any other teachers they had ever heard before. For others, His miracles were especially convincing. Still others were persuaded that He was the predicted Messiah spoken of in the Old Testament. After His death, many more people were impressed by His resurrection. It was unquestionably the major factor, as we have already seen.

> What drove early believers to trust Jesus?

We are interested in this chapter with what drove early believers to trust Jesus. This book is not the place to argue the rather complicated philosophical and theological background to such a thesis.[1] Rather, our attention will be more centered on the mind-set of the individuals who actually heard and accepted Jesus' message: why were they convinced of the truthfulness of His teachings? Certainly the chief factor was the activity of the Holy Spirit. But the New Testament states that this conviction was not created in a vacuum; different details appealed to different people, at least in getting their attention. The Holy Spirit used these items.

JESUS' UNIQUE CLAIMS

Jesus was certainly not a typical Jewish preacher or prophet. He repeatedly astounded those who heard His messages, and successfully broke the expected mold conjured up by both friend and foe alike. The major element in these surprising developments was the unique claims that Jesus made, as well as the things that He did. Clearly no other man spoke or acted in such a manner.

First of all, Jesus said some astounding things about Himself. His favorite self-designation was "Son of Man." Because this title could mean more than one thing, we have to see how Jesus used it. He applied it to His own ministry, such as when He claimed to forgive sins and was called a blasphemer (Mark 2:1-12). He also used it to predict His coming death and resurrection (Mark 8:31; 9:31). Lastly, He used the title to refer to His coming in judgment to set up God's Kingdom (Mark 13:26).

This last usage is highly reminiscent of Daniel 7:13-14, where the Son of Man was a preexistent Jewish apocalyptic figure who descended to earth at the time of the end to initiate God's Kingdom. He is given glory and a kingdom, and everyone will serve Him (v. 14). In fact, in Mark 14:61-64, Jesus seemed to be citing this passage in Daniel when he answered the high priest con-

> It was plain to the Jewish leaders that Jesus was claiming to be Deity.

cerning His identity. Once again, He is blamed with uttering blasphemy and this time He is condemned to die. It was plain to the Jewish leaders what Jesus was claiming.

38   The Truthfulness of Jesus' Teachings

Additionally, Jesus also referred to Himself by the lofty title "Son of God" or simply "Son" while speaking about the Father (Matt. 11:27; Mark 13:32). A special insight into Jesus' thinking here is supplied by His use of the term "Abba" to refer to His Father (Mark 14:36), which is an Aramaic word that might even be translated "Daddy." Used in the way Jesus did, this practice was without clear parallel in the Jewish literature of this period. He claimed a familiarity with the God of the universe that was simply not the accepted concept in Judaism, where God's name was frequently not even spoken in order to insure the proper respect.

To refer to God, the Creator of the universe, in the personalized ways that Jesus did constitutes clear assertions to being Deity. In the Jewish context, to claim to be God's Son was to make oneself equal to God, which was nothing short of blasphemous. This is how His countrymen understood Him (John 5:18; cf. John 10:30–33).

Second, Jesus claimed an authority unlike anything the Jews had contemplated before. Other prophets spoke of God's way of salvation, but Jesus said that He actually *was* that salvation: eternal life could be found *only* in Him.[2] It is widely recognized by scholars today that Jesus' central message involved His being God's instrument of salvation for the coming Kingdom: how individuals responded personally to Jesus and His teachings determined how they would fare at the final judgment (Mark 8:34-38; Matt. 25:31-46).

Another sign of His authority was that Jesus not only challenged long-standing and influential Jewish scholarship, but He placed His authority above their tradition. When He interpreted the Old Testament, He spoke from God's perspective (Matt. 5:20-48; Mark 2:23-28; 3:1-6).

The Truthfulness of Jesus' Teachings 39

Third, Jesus' actions confirmed His words and reinforced His claims. He absolutely infuriated the Jewish leaders by pronouncing that a man's sins were forgiven. But then Jesus healed the man, which He said was a demonstration that He had the authority to forgive sins (Mark 2:1-12). The teachers of the law recognized that, since only God could forgive sin, Jesus was guilty of blasphemy (vv. 6-7).

Another aspect from which to view Jesus' activities is that He often fulfilled Old Testament messianic prophecy. The best case can be made for those predictions that are clearly messianic and could not have been manipulated, such as Jesus' birth in Bethlehem (Micah 5:2), His miracles (Isa. 35:1-6), the specific time of His death (Dan. 9:24-27), intricate details concerning His death (Ps. 22; Isa. 53), as well as both His resurrection (Ps. 16:10) and exaltation (Isa. 52:13-15). More than one passage refers to the Messiah being Deity (Isa. 9:6-7; Dan. 7:13-14; Micah 5:2).[3]

Backing up these three areas regarding Jesus' claims and actions, we have a final indication of Who Jesus thought He was: the reactions of those who heard Him. The Jews of His time were in the best position to know what occurred; both friends and enemies agreed that He had taught and acted in a unique manner.

> Jesus often fulfilled OT messianic prophecy.

We've already seen a few examples of this from those who rejected Jesus' message. The Jewish leaders who heard Him forgive the lame man's sins declared His proclamation to be blasphemous. The most stunning case occurred when Jesus stood before the High Priest and was asked if He was the Christ (Messiah), the Son of God (Mark 14:61-64). Jesus plainly replied that He was ("I am"), thereby provoking the response from the

High Priest that He was guilty of blasphemy. Then He was condemned to death. On at least two other occasions, Jews tried to kill Him for claiming to be equal to God (John 5:17-18; 10:31-33,39).

An opposite response was given by the apostles and others who believed Jesus' words. Some of these were actually present during these times and knew Him the best. All of them agreed in calling Him the Son of God, Lord, Christ, and even God.[4]

There are a number of angles, then, from which to view the lofty claims and actions of Jesus. His self-designations, His personal claims to authority, and His actions all paint a unique picture. Further, both enemies as well as friends agreed on the fact that He said and did things that were the prerogative of God alone. Even in the history of religions, the founders of other major creeds did not make the unique claims that Jesus did.[5]

> Jesus' self-designations, His personal claims to authority, and His actions all paint a unique picture.

But anyone can make claims. History is full of misguided individuals, whether sincere or otherwise, who thought they were a "cut above" ordinary people. As we will see, even Scripture tells us to check out those who make declarations like these. So, as simply as we can put it, how do we know that Jesus was who He claimed to be?

JESUS' VIEW OF HIS MIRACLES

Jesus made many statements about Himself that can only be fairly interpreted as claims to being Deity. Further, He thought that He was on a specific mission from God, sent to act and speak for His Father. His message is unique when compared to

The Truthfulness of Jesus' Teachings

those whose teachings started the major world religions. But He gave no indication of being some misguided or crazed individual. His personal authority and the exemplary life He lived both had profound impacts on others. He is the most influential moral Teacher who ever lived — the only religious Teacher who is honored by those in each of the world's other religions. Add to this that He fulfilled numerous prophecies. Did Jesus provide any other reasons for believing His claims to be true?

We have said that this is not an apologetics text, so we will not produce a detailed argument here. But Jesus' own position on these matters seems quite clear.

(1) **True miracles, by their very nature, tend to evidence great power.** They seem to point beyond themselves. Traditionally, miracles confirm a religious message of some sort. Jesus believed this, too: miracles both indicated the presence of power and pointed to religious messages beyond themselves. This is why Satan's messengers also did miracles in order to mislead persons on behalf of their own evil agendas (Matt. 24:23-26). On the other hand, the prophecy that Jesus fulfilled and the miracles He did also pointed beyond themselves to His message.

> True miracles, by their very nature, tend to evidence great power.

(2) **Jesus taught that His miracles indicated that God approved of His message.**[6] This is generally admitted by critical scholars, too. Jesus said that healing a lame man showed that He had the authority to forgive sins (Mark 2:10). Another time, He told a group of unbelieving Jews that His miracles indicated that He was the Son of God (John 10:36-38). Most crucially, He said that His resurrection, in particular, would be the chief sign that His teachings were true.[7]

The Truthfulness of Jesus' Teachings

(3) **Jesus' followers testified that His miracles could show only one thing — that God was with Him.** Even His critics agreed that miracles evidenced special powers. But since they could not disprove Jesus' miracles, rather than believe in Him, they were forced to attribute the power to Satan. Jesus responded that if His power came from Satan, then it made no sense for Him to cast out demons, since He would be working against His own best interests (Matt. 12:22-29). We'll continue this point in detail in the next section by showing further why Jesus' miracles could only be explained by God approving His message.

GOD'S STAMP OF APPROVAL

Why did Jesus' Jewish listeners, both friends and foes, agree that miracles point beyond themselves to a religious message? We've said that this tends to be a characteristic of miracles themselves — they evidence great power. But beyond this, the Old Testament instructed them to observe carefully the message behind the events.

For this, we need to notice some items from a couple of crucial texts. In Deuteronomy 18:18-22, God presented a contrast between a true prophet whom God would raise up in the future (w. 18-19) and false prophets who do not speak for God (w. 20-22). In the first case, the true prophet would be sent by God and would speak His words; those who reject the prophet would be held accountable.

> The true prophet would be sent by God and would speak His words; those who reject the prophet would be held accountable.

In the second case, false prophets were to be

The Truthfulness of Jesus' Teachings

recognized on opposite grounds: if what they predicted did not come to pass, it would be known that they did not speak for God. The predictions of true prophets, then, come to pass. The Lord also gave criteria for those who performed miracles (Deut. 13:1-5).

It is in light of Old Testament teachings like these that Jews would judge Jesus: was He a true prophet of God, or not? What about His own predictions — like His resurrection[8] or the fall of Jerusalem (Luke 21:23-24)? Each of these was fulfilled. Further, since God would have had to be the One who raised Jesus, they could be assured that He would not raise a heretic from the dead. After all, Satan could not create life. Jesus' resurrection, then, was taken as the mightiest of signs that He was God's Spokesman. This was Jesus' view, and this is precisely how several New Testament passages also argue.

> Jesus' resurrection was the apex at which all the other prophets were pointing.

In the first sermon given after Jesus' ascension, Peter asserted that God had shown His approval of Jesus by the miracles that He did, and by His resurrection, in particular (Acts 2:22-24). This event served as the chief indication of God's commendation.

Later, Peter applies the Deuteronomy 18:18-19 passage directly to Jesus in Acts 3:21-23, stating that He was that prophet predicted by Moses and that, as such, God would hold people responsible by their response to His words. In fact, Peter said that Jesus' resurrection was the apex at which all the other prophets were pointing (3:24-26).

We have already mentioned two examples from Paul's preaching and teaching. In Acts 17:31 the resurrection was proclaimed to be the chief authentication of the Christian message. First

Corinthians 15:12-20 is a very clear and detailed statement of the centrality of Jesus' resurrection for Christian theology as a whole: without it there is nothing left to salvage. But since He was raised, all the other truth follows as well.

Other Pauline texts add to this perspective. A very important passage that is crucially important for our discussion is Romans 1:3,4. Like 1 Corinthians 15:3ff, this is another oral tradition of early origin, reflecting the earliest Christian preaching. This text states that Jesus was both a human being (by virtue of His incarnation), and Deity. He was shown (or declared) to be the Son of God, Christ (Messiah), and Lord by virtue of His resurrection from the dead.[9] Paul also explains that Jesus' death and resurrection made Him the Lord of both the dead and the living (Rom. 14:9).

Paul is not saying in Romans 1:3-4 that Jesus was only Deity after His resurrection. Rather, he was explaining that the resurrection was God's *public demonstration* of Jesus' Deity. Against the backdrop of the Jewish prophetic context, the resurrection revealed that Jesus really was Who He had already claimed to be from the outset. Here the idea is very similar to the one developed in this chapter: the earliest believers recognized that Jesus' unique statements about Himself were more than just claims. The resurrection had shown that these three lofty Christological titles (Son of God, Christ, Lord) were accurate, truthful designations for Him.

Another instance is John 20:31, where the reader is told that Jesus is both Christ and the Son of God. The miracles recorded in

The Truthfulness of Jesus' Teachings

this Gospel (and especially the resurrection appearances that John had just finished describing) were included for the express purpose of encouraging people to respond in faith to Jesus so that they might receive eternal life. So the author thought that these miracles should encourage belief in a unique Savior.

Peter declares that the Lord Jesus Christ's resurrection secured heaven for believers. Therefore, we don't need to be anxious for our future and can even rejoice in the face of persecution, knowing that this great event guarantees where we will spend eternity (1 Pet. 1:3-9).

It is the unified voice of the New Testament both that Jesus literally rose from the dead and that this event provided full and final verification of His unique claims. Although we have not pursued this line of argumentation in the detailed manner of an apologetic argument, the New Testament reasoning is solid. Jesus' teachings were verified by His resurrection from the dead.

> We don't need to be anxious for our future and can even rejoice in the face of persecution, knowing that this great event guarantees where we will spend eternity.

In conclusion, the only time that a bodily resurrection is known to have occurred,[10] it happened to the very Person who made these unique claims concerning His own Deity and His special mission from God. It is reasonable that Jesus would be in the best position to explain the significance of this event. He taught that His resurrection, as the chief miracle, verified the truthfulness of His teachings even beyond His earlier miracles and fulfilled prophecy. In brief, the unique resurrection event provided full and final confirmation of His unique self-claims and message.[11]

APPLICATION

The New Testament writers obviously considered the conclusion that Jesus Christ was raised from the dead to be of very great importance. This judgment also has great implications for believers today.

First, as God's chosen Spokesman, Jesus' teachings are true. The importance of this ought not be underestimated. In an age that questions truth, to know and understand Jesus' teaching about a subject is to know truth. So Christians have an obligation to study these teachings with a view toward learning and applying them. Of course, this question is not always an easy one — but just knowing that Jesus' teachings are true is a weighty conclusion.

Second, we ought not miss the significance of this with regard to the Person of Jesus. Since the resurrection shows that Jesus is Lord, Christians ought to submit to Him in all areas of their lives. We are not to study His words and then pick and choose what we wish to accept. Believers need to be committed to Jesus as their Lord, and not only in doctrinal areas, but also in ethical and practical ones, too. But this topic is more properly the subject for our companion volume on applying the truth of Jesus' resurrection.

Third, it may have been noticed throughout this chapter that the two most prominent themes that Jesus and New Testament writers especially emphasized as being verified by the resurrection were Jesus' Deity and His salvation message. We discussed the first subject here, largely by listing some of Jesus' own unique claims and the titles that the writers ascribed to Him. The subject of salvation is the special emphasis of the next chapter.

Returning briefly to the question at the beginning of this chapter, Christians do not have a product without a warranty. The stamp

The Truthfulness of Jesus' Teachings 47

of approval for our eternal life is clearly placed on our faith by the God of the universe. Could there possibly be a better guarantee?

NOTES

1. The interested reader who desires further details can see Gary R. Habermas, *The Resurrection of Jesus: An Apologetic* (Grand Rapids: Baker, 1980; Lanham: University Press of America, 1984), especially Chapters 2–5. A brief summary can be found in Habermas and Flew, *Did Jesus Rise?* pp. 39–42.

2. For some examples, see Mark 2:17; 10:45; Matt. 19:29; Luke 19:10; John 5:19,36; 14:6.

3. For some detailed studies of key prophecies, see Robert C. Newman, editor, *The Evidence of Prophecy* (Hatfield: International Biblical Research Institute, 1988), especially Chapters 9–11; Kenny Barfield, *The Prophet Motive: Examining the Reliability of the Biblical Prophets* (Nashville: Gospel Advocate, 1995), especially Section IV.

4. For some examples where these titles are used, respectively, see John 20:31; Acts 9:20; Gal 2:20; 1 John 4:15 (Son of God); 1 Cor. 2:3; Phil 2:11; Heb. 1:10; 13:20 (Lord); Acts 2:36; Eph. 5:1-2; Phil 2:11; 1 Pet. 3:18 (Christ); John 1:1; 20:28; Titus 2:13; Heb. 1:8; 2 Pet. 1:1 (God).

5. For some comparisons to other religions, see Norman Anderson, *Christianity and World Religions: The Challenge of Pluralism* (Leicester: InterVarsity Press, 1984); Stephen Neill, *Christian Faith and Other Faiths* (Oxford: Oxford University Press, 1970; Downers Grove, IL: InterVaristy, 1984); Stephen Neill, *The Supremacy of Jesus* (Downers Grove, IL: InterVarsity, 1984).

6. See Matt. 11:1-6; John 10:25; 11:41-42; 14:11; 15:24, plus the other examples listed in the text.

7. Matt. 12:38-40; 16:1-4; John 2:18-22.

8. For many of these predictions, see Matt. 12:38-40; 16:1-4,21; 17:22–23; Mark 8:31; 9:9,30-32; 10:33-34; 14:27-28; John 2:18-22; 14:19-20,28; 16:5-7,16-22,28. Jesus also predicted His death (by itself) in John 12:23-33, 17:11 and His future exaltation (by itself) in Mark 12:10-11,36; 14:62; John 13:31-36.

9. This passage is reminiscent of another early proclamation (Phil. 2:6-7) where Paul asserts that Jesus was both the essence (or nature) of God (*en morphei theou*) and the essence (or nature) of a human servant (*morphen doulou*).

10. On the uniqueness of Jesus' resurrection when compared to non-Christian religions, see Gary R. Habermas, "Resurrection Claims in Non-Christian Religions," *Religious Studies*, Vol. 25 (1989), pp. 167–177.

11. For the details of such an argument, see the sources in endnote 1 above.

SUGGESTED READINGS

Craig, William Lane. *Knowing the Truth about the Resurrection: Our Response to the Empty Tomb.* Revised Edition. Ann Arbor: Servant Books, 1988. Chapter 7.

Habermas, Gary R. *The Resurrection of Jesus: An Apologetic.* Grand Rapids: Baker, 1980; Lanham: University Press of America, 1984. Chapters 2–3.

Miller, Laurence W. *Jesus Christ Is Alive.* Boston: W.A. Wilde Company, 1949. Chapters II–III.

Milligan, William. *The Resurrection of Our Lord.* London: Macmillan, 1899. Lecture IV.I–II.

Sparrow-Simpson, W.J. *The Resurrection and the Christian Faith.* Grand Rapids: Zondervan, 1911, reprint 1968. Chapter XVIII.

Reflecting on Lesson Three

1. In your own words, what is it about the power of miracles that points beyond itself to a religious message? Can you give several indications?

2. What criteria could you suggest for telling the difference between a miraculous act by Satan or one by God? List or name some characteristics of each, especially considering that one of Satan's chief weapons is counterfeiting the real thing.

The Truthfulness of Jesus' Teachings

3. For group discussion: If you were a Jew listening to Jesus' message, how would you evaluate Him against the teachings of the Old Testament? What about His claims to Deity and the only way to salvation? How many times would you have to hear Him before being ready to believe?

4. For group discussion: How is Jesus' message unique? In particular, what about His teachings concerning Himself and salvation? From what you know of the teachings of other religions, how were Jesus' teachings different?

5. For group action: Pick two people to play the roles of a Christian and a non-Christian in a witnessing situation. Let the Christian start the conversation. What approach would you take in speaking to someone from another faith? Would you start with the unique teachings of Jesus? How about the resurrection? Try several approaches and discuss which ones seemed to work best.

6. How would you answer someone who said that Jesus was not the only way to God, even though Jesus did teach this? How would you try to convince them of the New Testament position?

Consider this:

The man, Jesus, claimed unequivocally to be God. This is a truly astounding proposition. To prepare for lesson four, meditate on this idea in depth. How does it affect your assurance of salvation? If we accept His claim for Himself, how does this fact play out in the way we live our lives on a day-to-day basis?

4
SALVATION

In this lesson:
- What constitutes the gospel
- The role of faith in salvation
- Jesus' teachings about the Kingdom
- What the death, burial, and resurrection mean to us

Amber was clearly troubled when she came to talk. Bothered about the assurance of her salvation, she had done everything she could think of in order to be sure that she was a believer. "I've prayed to God about trusting Christ as my Savior many, many times. I just want to be sure," she proclaimed.

"Why have your questions centered on this issue?" I asked her.

"It's very simple," she countered, clearly having thought this all through before. "My salvation is the most important thing in the world to me. So I examine it from every possible angle just to be positive that I am not deceiving myself."

Few subjects are closer to the hearts of Christians than this one. After all, the biblical means of salvation is the key to eternal life. As we just observed in the last chapter, this is a topic that was given special consideration by both Jesus and the New Testament writers who linked it, in particular, with the confirmation provided by Jesus' resurrection. In fact, the argument that was probably the most frequently used to encourage unbelievers to trust Christ is that He was raised from the dead.

THE CONTENT OF THE GOSPEL

Perhaps the clearest statement of the content of the gospel is found in the early Christian confession in 1 Corinthians 15:1-4. After stating that accepting the gospel and holding fast to it is sufficient to save a person (vv. 1-2), Paul singles out several facts. He asserts that Christ died for our sins, He was buried, He rose again from the dead, and appeared to a number of people in agreement with the Scriptures (vv. 3ff).

In this text, Paul lists at least five facts that comprise the gospel. At a minimum, the gospel includes the Deity of Jesus (as indicated by the title "Christ"

> Central facts of the gospel
> in 1 Cor. 15:3ff.:
> 1. Christ is deity.
> 2. He died for our sins.
> 3. He was buried.
> 4. He rose from the dead.
> 5. He was seen by many witnesses.

Resurrection: Heart of New Testament Doctrine

52   Salvation

instead of by His proper name),[1] His atoning death, His burial, His resurrection, and His appearances. The last four facts are tied together by Paul's use of the connecting words "and that," linking them together as a unit. Interestingly, although they are implied, Paul never again separates Jesus' burial or appearances in his discussions of the gospel.

Paul summarizes his gospel message in a few other places, too. He again quotes an early Christian confession in 2 Timothy 2:8. He contrasts Jesus' humanity and His Deity: He is of the lineage of David, but He is also referred to by His title "Christ." He was raised from the dead, too. Again, As Paul continues further, speaking of the salvation and eternal glory available in Christ Jesus, he returns to the subjects of His death and resurrection (2:10-11).

Paul also refers to the message of the gospel a chapter earlier (2 Tim. 1:8-11). He mentions Jesus' destruction of death and His offer of immortality to those who respond, both of which depend on Jesus' death and resurrection, as Paul says elsewhere (such as 1 Cor. 15:1-4,54-57). Once again, Jesus is also called Savior and Christ.

> Christians are those who respond to God's grace and exercise faith in Him.

Paul begins the Book of Romans by identifying the gospel he preached: Jesus was born with a human nature and was also shown to be the Son of God, Christ, and Lord by His resurrection from the dead (1:1-4). Christians are those who respond to God's grace and exercise faith in Him (1:6-7).

Paul expands his treatment of the gospel in Romans 10. Here he informs his readers that anyone who confesses the Lordship of Jesus and believes in their hearts that God raised Him from the dead will be saved (v. 9).[2]

Salvation

In each of these passages, Paul includes a common core of facts. Every text either specifically names the Deity of Jesus, or at least mentions one of His divine titles, like Christ, Lord, or Son of God. Paul is quite clear in Romans 10:9 that salvation consists of confessing Jesus as Lord. Each text also reports Jesus' death and resurrection. So I conclude that the gospel contains a *minimum* of at least three indispensable facts — the Deity, death, and resurrection of Jesus Christ.

We might also mention briefly that the gospel actually uses evidences within its formulation. At least in 1 Corinthians 15:3ff, Jesus' death is followed by His burial, while His resurrection is indicated by His appearances. In all of the gospel passages, the resurrection is included. So it is difficult to understand why some Christians would question the benefit of having good reasons for their faith when these cannot even be separated from the plan of salvation.

In the next section we will maintain that faith is not actually placed in the gospel facts themselves, as necessarily crucial as they are, but in the Jesus of the facts. In other words, saving faith is trusting a Person and what He did for us in history, not trusting history *per se*. Perhaps we might even say that we trust the Jesus *of* history. But we do not want to be misunderstood here. When faith is placed in the Person of Jesus Christ, it is understood that what He did for us in time and space is indispensable, according to Paul. To repeat, if Jesus was not raised, our faith gains nothing for us (1 Cor. 15:14,17).

> Saving faith is trusting a Person and what He did for us in history, not trusting history *per se*.

FAITH

We have concluded that the nature of the gospel includes the chief components of at least the death, resurrection, and Person of Jesus Christ. But the facts of the gospel do not stand alone in our gaining salvation. Otherwise a person could be saved simply by giving mental approval to this data. But the individual must trust the Person of Jesus Christ and what He did to atone for his sins. In other words, the biblical testimony is that faith placed in the Jesus of the gospel facts brings salvation (1 Cor. 15:1-2). Faith is a personal decision — it is trust in a Person.

> Faith is a personal decision—it is trust in a Person.

So there are two sides of the salvation equation here: Who Jesus is along with what He did for us, and how we respond to Him in faith. In other words, He did something and we need to respond with our trust. *Both* sides are indispensable. Having dealt with the content, we will now see the interaction between it and our faith.

The major Greek word for belief or faith (*pistis*) is stronger than its English equivalent. The kind of faith required by the New Testament is not merely mental agreement or mild acceptance of something (as in "I believe George Washington was the first president of the United States."). Actually, we already saw how this weak sort of faith was insufficient to save when certain Jews had a superficial faith in Jesus (John 2:23-25; cf. Acts 8:13,18-23). James tells us that the demons believe this way, too (Jas. 2:19), but they are not Christians. Rather, saving faith involves placing our confidence and trust in Jesus. It is surrendering to Him and relying upon Him for our salvation. He is our hope of heaven. In this sense, our faith has our most important desires and needs as its focal point.[3]

Salvation

The gospel facts are regularly cited as the grounds for our personal decision. Just like we shouldn't get married until we first get some background information, saying "I do" to Jesus is built on a foundation. Besides the many examples we gave above, John 20:30-31 is another text where the writer explains that there is something to believe. After a presentation of a few of Jesus' resurrection appearances, John tells us that he recorded some of Jesus' miracles for the purpose of encouraging faith in his readers.

The historical truthfulness of the gospel facts was the chief reason given in the early church in order to encourage a faith response. In one example, Peter recounted the gospel of the death and resurrection of Jesus and encouraged the Jewish leaders to hear his message of repentance and forgiveness of sins (Acts 5:29-32). Similar scenes recur repeatedly in the Book of Acts.[4] But we will just note here this connection between the factual content of the gospel and its use in encouraging individuals to turn to the Lord in faith.

Paul also uses this approach. Besides the examples in Acts, we have seen that Romans 10:9 makes the Deity, death, and resurrection of Jesus the grounds for belief and confession of the Lordship of Jesus. Paul also explains that belief in Jesus' Deity ("our Lord"), His atoning death, and resurrection are the means of experiencing justification (Rom. 4:24-25). Further, sinners who were once dead toward the Lord were raised to life along with Jesus, by God's grace (Eph. 2:1-5).

Peter adds that Christians are those who believe in God through Jesus Christ, trusting His atoning death and resurrection. This results in the believer's hope

> Belief in Jesus' Deity, His atoning death, and resurrection are the means of experiencing justification.

being placed in God (1 Peter 1:18-21). Later Peter states that Christians are saved by the resurrection of Jesus Christ (3:21-22).

Repeatedly in the New Testament, then, the gospel of the atoning death and resurrection of Jesus Christ is defined and declared to be the factual basis for an individual's belief. The Jesus of the gospel is the Subject of our faith, accounting for the individual's personal conversion and salvation. From start to finish, the resurrection is at the very center of the proclamation.

THE CENTRALITY OF THE GOSPEL

Virtually all scholars, whether liberal or conservative, agree that Jesus' central message was the Kingdom of God and its entrance requirements. So the preaching of salvation was the nucleus of Jesus' ministry. One way to determine this conclusion is to examine the statements Jesus made regarding the chief reason for His first coming.

Jesus repeatedly taught that His call to Kingdom life and the essential prerequisite of salvation was the focus of His message. For instance, He said that He came for the purpose of seeking and saving the lost (Luke 19:10); to call sinners to repentance (Mark 2:17); to give His life as a ransom for many (Mark 10:45); and to provide eternal life for His followers (John 10:10,27-28). We are also told that Jesus' was sent to provide forgiveness of sins (Matt. 1:21); that He shed His blood for that purpose (Matt. 26:28); that He came to provide the possibility of everlasting life (John 3:14-16); and that He was given authority to grant eternal life (John 17:2).

In almost every one of these passages, it is made plain that the purpose of Jesus' Incarnation was to preach the message of the gospel, inviting people into His eternal Kingdom. Sometimes a different angle is emphasized, but Jesus repeatedly announced

Salvation

the chief nature of His message as proclaiming the gospel of the Kingdom.

Even *after* His resurrection from the dead, Jesus continued to announce this same central teaching. He taught His disciples to preach repentance and the forgiveness of sins (Luke 24:46-48), emphasizing the making of disciples and teaching His words (Matt. 28:18-20). He sent His disciples the same way His Father sent Him (John 20:21), proclaiming a blessing on those who would believe (John 20:29). Luke tells us that during the 40 days of Jesus' appearances, He both provided incredible evidences that He was alive and continued to instruct His disciples concerning the Kingdom of God (Acts 1:3). Later, when Jesus appeared to Paul, He called him to preach the same message.[5]

> The purpose of Jesus' Incarnation was to preach the message of the gospel, inviting people into His eternal Kingdom.

Other New Testament authors also identified the centrality of Jesus' gospel message of the Kingdom. John interpreted Jesus' announcement of a blessing on those who believe (John 20:29) in terms of a general invitation to exercise faith unto eternal life (20:30-31). Peter pointed out that, after His resurrection, Jesus commanded His disciples to preach His message, promising forgiveness of sins to all who believe (Acts 10:39-43). Paul noted that he and the other apostles were witnesses to Jesus and the gospel, offering forgiveness to those who exercise belief (Acts 13:28-39). Other texts teach similarly (Heb. 2:3-4; 9:28; 1 John 1:2).

Therefore, Jesus' major message was the Kingdom of God and the requirements of salvation. This is true of Jesus' teachings both before and after His resurrection. Further, the New Testament writers as a whole agree in this assessment.[6]

APPLICATION

There is widespread agreement among believers that the nature of the gospel and its appropriation by faith is at the very heart of Christianity. Several lessons to learn and remember follow from the centrality of this message.

First, Christians should never lose sight of the centrality of the gospel, both theoretically (in its proper formulation) and practically (in its clear proclamation). There are constant pressures to compromise or dilute the gospel, or to subordinate it to other concerns. For example, the current popularity of religious toleration has only added to an already existing number of attempts to subtract all uniqueness from the Christian message and to interpret it in terms of some general, ethereal "religiosity." We hear that the original proclamation of Christianity is similar to what all religions hold. Such reductions of our crucial content must be opposed by the believer, sometimes on different levels. It might be pointed out that these are invalid interpretations of the texts in question,[7] that Jesus taught a unique message among the worlds' religions, and that the gospel facts are heavily evidenced.

> Jesus taught a unique message among the worlds' religions.

Another instance of keeping the gospel central occurs in the question of whether the Christian ought to be more concerned about giving the good news or with getting involved in the lives of needy persons. Initially, it should be acknowledged that *both* areas are *crucially* important and are not necessarily opposed to one another at all.

But it is still true that it is sometimes necessary to choose an

Salvation 59

emphasis between the two, and here Jesus' own instruction should be heeded. He taught us to place our devotion to God first and our efforts to assist fellow human beings second. He said these were the two greatest commands (Matt. 22:34-40; Luke 10:25-38). It is clear, then, that we should be concerned about both emphases. Even though involvement with the needs of others is second to one's love for God and sharing that message, it is more important than many other Christian activities. Jesus continued His teaching by telling the parable of the Good Samaritan (Luke 10:30-37), with the theme of being willing to sacrifice even for those whom society considers repulsive. Jesus' conclusion is that we should "Go and do likewise" (v. 37).

I think the proper principle is that the gospel ought to receive priority, but this does not necessarily translate into the actual minutes spent on each of these two great commands, or mean that the gospel must be given before anything else is done. Sometimes we need to earn the right to be heard; even Jesus healed before He preached. But these concerns should never cause us to neglect the communication of the good news. Explaining God's path to eternal life remains of primary importance. In brief, there is always a need for radical involvement with *both* people's spiritual and material needs, although we need to keep the priority that Jesus commanded us.

> Explaining God's path to eternal life remains of primary importance.

So the gospel needs to keep its centrality just as it did with Jesus. This extends even to issues such as written and oral presentations of the good news. Too often, tracts and presentations of the "sinner's prayer" leave out the resurrection, for example, as if the cross is the full extent of the gospel. We need to be faithful to the New Testament teaching and be as clear as it is on this subject.

Second, the gospel reveals at least three intensely practical truths concerning God's relation to us. The Cross (and the Incarnation in general) shows that **God is personally involved in our lives**. He is not aloof. He is not a God who has removed Himself from the world. After all, He sent His only Son to provide for our deepest needs. He does care for us. As God, Jesus Himself was also intimately concerned about the problems of individuals. He repeatedly showed compassion towards the sick, poor, societal outcasts, as well as children, His disciples, and even His enemies.

Additionally, the Cross is the **ultimate expression of love** in all of history. We could never even comprehend the depth of God's perfect and eternal love for His only Son. Yet this divine relationship did not keep Jesus from willingly sacrificing His life for our sins, or His Father from sending Him. The purpose of Jesus' death was to reconcile us to Him. And all the while, we were living in sin, apart from Him.

> We can say that we don't understand why we suffer, but we have no right to conclude that He doesn't understand or care about our pain.

Finally, Jesus' crucifixion reveals **God's understanding of our deepest pain** like no other occurrence could. He watched His only Son suffer excruciating, torturous pain, finally even dying for man's sin, of which He was never even guilty, and in which He never took part. It has been said that crucifixion may involve the worst suffering of all. We can say that *we* don't understand why we suffer, but we have no right to conclude that *He* doesn't understand or care about our pain.

Resurrection: Heart of New Testament Doctrine

Salvation 61

The gospel is the very center of Christianity. The truth of the cross ensures the truth of the Christian message and the essential difference between Christianity and all other belief systems. It reveals that God's way is to reach us (not vice versa). He is intricately involved with our deepest needs and He loves people far more than we love others, or even ourselves. He has had firsthand experience with ultimate pain. Perhaps most importantly, He triumphed supremely in His resurrection and exaltation.

Thirdly, not only is the gospel of the Kingdom Jesus' central message, but there is a strong, twofold confirmation of this truth based on the resurrection. In other words, when Jesus was raised from the dead, He provided two strong arguments for the eternal life that He was preaching.

Initially, we have **indirect verification**. Since Jesus' teachings are truthful (as pointed out in Chapter Three), then God's confirmation *especially* extends to the gospel, since it was His major message. In other words, if God verified anything at all in Jesus' message by raising Him from the dead, then this evidence would most definitely single out His teaching about eternal life above all else, since Jesus came chiefly to preach that truth. Briefly stated, we can be most sure about the content of the gospel and the truth of eternal life because it was His central message.

Further, we also have **direct confirmation**. The resurrection of Jesus in a glorified body is the only miracle of which it can be said that, by its very nature, it requires the truth of heaven. While the feeding of the 5,000, for example, does not demand an afterlife, Jesus' resurrection directly reveals it. When the disciples saw the resurrected Jesus, they saw what we might call walking, talking, eternal life.

> When the disciples saw the resurrected Jesus, they saw what we might call walking, talking, eternal life.

For forty days, heaven broke into history in the Person of the resurrected Jesus! His followers witnessed a foretaste of heaven!

Thus Jesus' teachings on the gospel are specially verified both in that God, by raising Jesus from the dead, approved of His central message as being of primary importance and also because the resurrection is actually a true-to-life example of heaven. The nature and centrality of the gospel and the need for conversion are the central teachings of Christianity. That such doctrines are so strongly evidenced is yet a further indication of God's grace. The believer needs to insist that these doctrines continue to have the same centrality and premier importance that they had for Jesus, the apostles, and the earliest church.

Fourth, this eternal life is a possession that begins in the present and extends all the way into the future Kingdom of God. Its initial blessings are available to us right now (John 6:47; 1 John 5:13). For example, the power of the resurrected Jesus indwells us through the Holy Spirit, making it possible to choose God over sin (Phil. 3:10). And Jesus taught that the Christian's present possession of eternal life was even relevant when loved ones died (John 11:25-26).[8] Believers have begun a new life that takes us right into eternity (John 5:24).

NOTES

1. Although in this first text Jesus' Deity is not specifically singled out like the other four facts, Paul does use the title "Christ." In other passages (see discussion below), Paul does specify the importance of the Deity of Jesus when becoming a Christian (cf. Rom. 1:3-4; 10:9; 1 Cor. 12:3).

2. Some scholars think that this particular confession is actually a baptismal creed, where the candidate declared his faith before or during the baptism itself. There is a contrast here between the frequent practice used today where the minister simply asks a question or two and the individual answers in the affirmative, and that in the early church where the person apparently

Salvation

did the talking. For the New Testament practice, see Acts 22:16 where Paul was told to call on the Lord's name in baptism, and John's baptism in Matt. 3:6, where the candidates confessed their sins while being baptized.

3. For a readable definition of the Greek terms and their usages, see W.E. Vine, *An Expository Dictionary of New Testament Words*, four volumes (Old Tappan: Fleming H. Revell, 1966), vol. I, pp. 116-117, 211-212.

4. See Chapter 2, endnote 1, for a list of several such scenarios. We will treat these passages in more detail in *The Resurrection: Heart of the Christian Life* when dealing with the subject of evangelism.

5. Rom. 1:1,5; 11:13; Gal. 1:1,11-12; 2:7-9; 1 Tim. 2:7; 2 Tim. 1:10-11.

6. However, this is not to say that the Kingdom of God and eternal life are synonymous. For example, such life was a possibility for Old Testament saints before the initiation of the Kingdom brought about by Jesus' preaching.

7. Issues like these sometimes involve the proper application of the rules of interpretation (hermeneutics). In this case, there are literally dozens of texts that can be analyzed, defined, and cross-referenced for a clearer indication of the author's meaning.

8. The availability to the believer of resurrection power to conquer sin and deal with grief are two more subjects that are addressed in *The Resurrection: Heart of the Christian Life.*

SUGGESTED READINGS

Gaffin, Jr., Richard. *Resurrection and Redemption: A Study in Paul's Soteriology.* Second Edition. Phillipsburg: Presbyterian and Reformed, 1978.

Habermas, Gary R. *The Resurrection of Jesus: An Apologetic.* Grand Rapids: Baker, 1980; Lanham: University Press of America, 1984. Chapter 5.

Milligan, William. *The Resurrection of Jesus.* London: Macmillan, 1899. Lecture IV.II.

Sparrow-Simpson, W.J. *The Resurrection and the Christian Faith.* Grand Rapids: Zondervan, 1911, reprint 1968. Chapter XX.

Tenney, Merrill C. *The Reality of the Resurrection.* New York: Harper and Row, 1963. Chapter VII.

64   **Salvation**

Reflecting on Lesson Four

1. Make a list of indispensable doctrines that belong in any presentation of the gospel facts. Provide texts for each. Then defend your choices. Why is each one necessary?

2. Write out a definition of faith. Make sure you understand the strength of the word as it is used in the New Testament. How is it related to the facts of the gospel?

3. Why is it so important that the Kingdom of God and the entrance requirements of salvation are the center of Jesus' teachings? Write down and review some of the implications.

4. Gather a number of gospel tracts. Examine carefully the way they present the gospel. Did you find all of the necessary facts? Was the resurrection always mentioned? (Or make this a group activity where you try to locate tracts that do not present the entire gospel. Share your findings with the other members.)

5. For group discussion: What priorities should Christians have in giving? Where does the primacy of the gospel fit in? How about giving to those in need? Does Galatians 6:10 provide any hints here? What does Jesus' teaching about the two greatest commands (Matt. 22:34-40) say about the importance of giving to these two causes?

6. Take a few minutes to meditate on the meaning of Jesus' crucifixion. In practical terms, what does the cross mean to you concerning God being personal, caring for you, and understanding your pain? Think carefully through each of these areas. How might meditating on the cross help

when you are tempted to think that God is impersonal? How about when you question His concern for your needs? Perhaps most of all, how can you be sure that God understands your pain even when you don't? Give several reasons for each.

Consider this:

In preparation for lesson five try to recall the things you were taught as a child about what you would be like after you had died and gone to heaven. From what you know as an adult Christian, were these pictures accurate? Develop a clear picture of what you think a believer's resurrection will be like and then read lesson five.

5

RAISED LIKE JESUS

In this lesson:
- Jesus' resurrection body
- The bodily resurrection of believers
- The Second Coming and other future events

"When you die, you go up to heaven and become an angel," said the kindly Sunday School teacher, obviously trying to paint a beautiful picture of the afterlife for an inquisitive young child.

"An angel?" I questioned.

"Yes — you will love it. Everything will be beautiful," was the response.

I thought about this for a minute. Visions of cherubs with

round faces and soft, fluttering wings filled my mind. They were always smiling but never getting to play football. I wasn't very impressed.

Sometimes we struggle when we try to explain to a child what we will look like after death. Too often, we fill in the gaps with incorrect features. While Scripture might not say as much as we might like concerning details of the afterlife, at least one question is answered repeatedly. We are given the blueprint for our resurrection bodies — and they are not patterned after the angels. We have a much higher calling!

More than any other doctrine in the New Testament, the resurrection of Jesus is tied to the Christian's resurrection. One day the believer's body will be raised like that of Jesus and death will forever be conquered. This promise of the New Testament is mentioned more than a dozen times.

> One day the believer's body will be raised like that of Jesus and death will forever be conquered.

We will begin with a study of the nature of Jesus' resurrection body. Then we will see what we can learn concerning the believer's future body. We will also discuss the relation between Jesus' resurrection and some other future events.

JESUS' RESURRECTION BODY

What was Jesus' body like after He was raised from the dead? Since the believer's resurrected body will be similar, this subject is an important one for us.

The most extensive descriptions of Jesus' resurrection appearances occur in the Gospels. We are clearly told that Jesus was raised from the dead and appeared in the same physical body in which He died on the cross.[1] Several considerations lead us to this conclusion. But this is not to say, however, that there were no changes at all. Just the fact that Jesus' body was no longer mortal requires an explanation.

Each of the synoptic Gospels begins its resurrection account with a description of the empty tomb and an angelic message for the women who arrive afterwards. They are told that Jesus was crucified, buried, and was now risen. The *same* Jesus who had died on the cross and was carefully placed in the tomb had now exited the premises (Matt. 28:5-6; Mark 16:6-7; Luke 24:4-7). The Book of Acts also reports the same process (Acts 2:23-32; 13:29-30,34-37).

In John, the women ("we," 20:2) also find the stone removed from the empty tomb. After hearing the news, Peter and John run to the tomb and examine it, discovering the graveclothes that Jesus had left behind (John 20:5-7; cf. Luke 24:12). John believed that Jesus had been raised (John 20:8-9).

> From the moment Jesus was first seen, the Gospels and Acts are clear that He appeared in a real body.

The chief indications of Jesus' physical nature after His resurrection from the dead come from His appearances. From the moment Jesus was first seen, the Gospels and Acts are also clear that He appeared in a real body. And He was recognized. Although God kept certain believers from identifying Him (Luke 24:16,31), the vast majority recognized Him immediately (cf. Matt. 28:9; John 20:20,26-28; 21:12).

Among His many appearances, He was touched on at least two occasions (Matt. 28:9-10; John 20:16-17).[2] A minimum of two other times He offered to be touched but we are not told if He actually was (Luke 24:39; John 20:27-29). In a very interesting passage, Ignatius, an early post-New Testament Christian author who wrote about A.D. 107-110, tells us that the disciples responded to Jesus' offer to touch Him and found that He indeed had a flesh and blood body (Smyrnaens 3).

Another indication of the corporeal nature of the appearances is that Jesus showed His followers that His resurrection body was the same one that died on the cross. He did this by letting them see His healed wounds. The

> The resurrected Jesus ate with His disciples on a few occasions.

first instance, on the day of His resurrection, was to the ten disciples who were fearfully gathered together (John 20:19-20; Luke 24:36-40). A week later, Jesus appeared to Thomas, who was absent on the earlier occasion, and showed him His body and its wounds (John 20:24-29).

Further, Jesus ate with His disciples on a few occasions, one more indication of the physical nature of His body. This occurred with the two followers with whom He walked to Emmaus, who recognized Him at the dinner table (Luke 24:28-31). Later, he ate in front of His disciples specifically to show them that He possessed a normal body (Luke 24:41-43). Then, in a seashore setting, He actually prepared breakfast for His disciples (John 21:8-14). Although we are not exactly told that Jesus ate with them this time, it is at least implied. Eating is mentioned twice more (Acts 1:4; 10:41), but we don't know whether or not these were repeats of earlier incidents.

Of all the Gospel passages that emphasize the physical resurrection body of Jesus, perhaps the major one is Luke 24:36-43.

When Jesus appeared to His startled disciples, they were scared and thought they were witnessing the presence of a disembodied ghost.

Jesus addressed these doubts with the straightforward claim that His flesh and bone body, and His crucifixion wounds in particular, clearly indicated that He was not a ghost. To further advance His claims, He asked for food and ate before their eyes. John adds that the disciples rejoiced at realizing that Jesus was indeed there with them (John 20:20).

So the first five New Testament books agree that the same Jesus who was dead and buried was now alive again in His own body. There are many indications of this. The empty tomb, the angelic messages, Jesus' appearances, including His being recognized, touched, showing His wounds, and eating all point to one important conclusion: there was *continuity* with Jesus' body before and after the cross.

Now a major question arises. What about the resurrection appearance to Paul? Some think that his experience on the road to Damascus was an objective encounter with the risen Jesus, but one that was a bodiless vision. But the relevant passages argue differently.

Luke provides the most details concerning Jesus' appearance to Paul, addressing the subject in three major texts (Acts 9:1-9; 22:5-11; 26:12-18). Paul was overcome by a light described as being brighter than that of the noontime sun, and he fell to the ground (9:3-4; 22:6-7; 26:13-14). He heard a voice speaking to him that identified Himself as Jesus (9:4-5; 22:7-8; 26:14-15). Paul, obviously much shaken, was blinded for three days (9:8-9; 22:11).

It is true that Paul's companions saw no one (9:7), as if in contrast to Paul. Neither were they blinded. Yet, such descriptions far too seldom underline the physical aspects to which all those

Raised Like Jesus 71

present were witnesses. Paul's friends also saw the light and likewise responded by falling to the ground (26:13-14). They also heard the sounds of the voice (9:7), though without perceiving the meaning (22:9)[3] and were startled, as well (9:7).

So while it seems that Paul's companions did not have exactly the same experience that he did, Luke tells us enough to make it clear that it is entirely inappropriate to say that Paul was the only one to experience what happened. There were real affects in the space-time world. Outward manifestations such as an unearthly light strong enough to prompt all of the men to fall down, along with some sort of voice, were apparent to all those who were present.

Another important point here is that Luke was unaware of any discrepancy whatsoever between Jesus' bodily appearances to the disciples in Luke 24 and the later appearance to Paul, which he detailed three times. Luke made no effort to change one to fit the other and obviously thought there was no need to do so. We can conclude that he did not see a problem between the two.

Further, we have Paul's own eyewitness testimony that he saw the risen Jesus (1 Cor. 9:1; 15:8). While he does not give us details in these texts concerning his appearance, he does address the subject elsewhere. In Acts 13:27-37 Paul presents a similar scenario to that of the Gospels: the same Jesus who was dead and buried was raised from the dead. And on two separate occasions Paul notes his position on the resurrection of the dead by identifying himself with the view held by the Pharisees (Acts 23:6; 26:4-8; cf. Phil. 3:4-6), who accepted a bodily resurrection (Acts 23:8).

> On two separate occasions Paul notes his position on the resurrection of the dead by identifying himself with the Pharisees.

Resurrection: Heart of New Testament Doctrine

72 Raised Like Jesus

Some may ask why Paul seems to say something different in 1 Corinthians 15:45,50. But in verse 45, it seems strange for Paul to be saying that Jesus was a disembodied spirit, when, in the very same sentence, he refers not to Adam's body but to his soul or life (*psychen zosan*). In other words, Paul refers to the body of *neither* Jesus nor Adam, so we cannot affirm that Jesus is bodiless without raising the same question about Adam. Besides, the previous verse (44) affirms both a natural body and a spiritual body, just as Paul does in Philippians 3:21.

In the second reference (15:50), "flesh and blood" is a common Semitic idiom referring to our mortal, temporal bodies. The phrase is sometimes translated "humans" or "people."[4] In other words, Paul is saying that believers cannot go to heaven in their mortal bodies; they must be resurrected. He is not trying to give us an anatomy lesson here! In this sense, the second portion of verse 50 naturally follows the train of thought in the first part: our perishable bodies must be made imperishable in order to actually experience God's eternal state. Paul is not even addressing the question concerning the composition of Jesus' or the believer's resurrected body. He is merely stating that we must be changed along the lines he has just mentioned in 15:42–44. Yet, there was still bodily continuity.

> Paul is saying that believers cannot go to heaven in their mortal bodies; they must be resurrected.

One other consideration should be mentioned here that may be the most important of all, even if we cannot provide details in this context. An investigation of Pauline anthropology, including a careful analysis of Paul's language, shows that he clearly taught that the resurrection body of both Jesus and that of believers will be physical in nature. Neither the appearance to him on the way to Damascus nor his commentary in 1 Corinthians 15 changes this conclusion.[5]

So the combined witness of the New Testament is that Jesus was raised in the same body in which He died. However, He was changed, at least in the sense that He was no longer mortal. He still bore the marks of the wounds because it really was His body. But now He was prepared for His life at the right hand of His Father. Later when He appeared to Paul, He had already ascended to heaven and was glorified. The blinding light was a manifestation of this. Paul refers to His body in its final state as "glorious" (Phil. 3:21). Now we are better prepared to see the relation between Jesus' resurrected body and that of believers.

THE BELIEVER'S RESURRECTION BODY

No doctrine in the entire New Testament is more closely or frequently connected to Jesus' resurrection than the resurrection of believers' bodies. The relationship between the two is mentioned more than a dozen times, occasionally in extended discourses.

Jesus made the connection in the context of telling His disciples that He would be leaving them soon. But He said that they would see Him again. It was precisely because He lived that they would also live (John 14:18-19). In John's typical fashion, this is probably a reference to both eternal life being the believer's present possession and extending later into a future reality through Jesus Christ (cf. John 5:24; 6:47; 1 John 5:13).

At Jesus' death, Matthew states that a number of tombs were opened and the dead were raised, appearing to many people in Jerusalem after Jesus' resurrection (Matt. 27:51-53). We are not

74 Raised Like Jesus

told whether these persons, like Lazarus, were raised to die again, or if they were the first ones after Jesus to appear in their resurrection bodies. Regardless, the clear meaning of the text is that this was a precursor to what would happen in the future at the resurrection of the dead, due to Jesus' resurrection.

Before turning to the epistles, a few references in the Book of Acts should be noted. When the disciples first began proclaiming the gospel after Pentecost, the Jewish priests and Sadducees were very much disturbed. What bothered them the most was that the disciples were teaching the resurrection of the dead, grounding the doctrine in the resurrection of Jesus (Acts 4:1-2). Apparently this connection between Jesus' resurrection (Acts 3:15,26) and the believer's (4:2) was a mainstay of their message and the Jewish leaders singled it out as a matter of concern. Later, Paul taught similarly by asserting that Jesus was the first to be raised, implying that others would follow (Acts 26:23).

Paul's language in Acts 26:23 brings to mind an issue that we will address briefly. Some, like Jehovah's Witnesses, claim that phrases where Jesus is called God's "firstborn" or "begotten" are indications that He was created by God at a specific point in time. But in Acts 13:32-33, God's having begotten Jesus is explained in terms of the resurrection. Other passages like Colossians 1:18 and Revelation 1:5 also define firstborn in terms of Jesus' resurrection. First Corinthians 15:20,23 does the same regarding the term "firstfruits." To be the "firstborn from the dead" (or "firstfruits"), then, indicates Jesus' preeminent place in the process of resurrection. He was also the first to be raised in a resurrection body, to be followed later by

> To be the "firstborn from the dead" indicates Jesus' preeminent place in the process of resurrection.

believers. These terms are also used in reference to Jesus' physical birth (John 1:14; Heb. 1:5-6). But at no time does Scripture ever teach that Jesus was created by God.[6]

An extended passage that links Jesus' resurrection to that of believers is 2 Corinthians 4:7-5:10. While speaking of the subjects of persecution, suffering, and death, Paul reminds his audience that the same God who raised Jesus from the dead will also raise up believers (4:14). After telling his readers that they ought to focus their thoughts on eternal life, Paul addresses what is widely taken to be the subject of the intermediate state — what will happen to believers immediately after death but before the resurrection of the body (5:1-9). Although this is a difficult passage, we might just mention the majority view that Paul is teaching that, at death, the believer will remain in a disembodied state until His body is resurrected. This in-between realm is still a blessed one, primarily because to leave the body means we will be present with Jesus (5:8).[7]

Philippians 1:21-23 is among the most important texts that also address the intermediate state. In straighforward language, Paul is clear that his death would be a benefit (*kerdos*, v. 21). Interestingly, Paul's word here indicates that his death would make him a profit. So should he prefer to live or die? Paul's response: "I desire to depart and be with Christ, which is better by far" (v. 23). Paul's choice of wording (*polloi mallon kreisson*), which might be translated "very much better,"[8] is a strongly qualified, passionate statement about the outstanding benefits of being with Christ. It seems as if he wanted his reader to understand that there was really no comparison here — dying and being in the presence of Christ was easily to be preferred.

The intermediate state is referred to in several other texts, as well. Jesus promised a conscious paradise that the believing thief on the cross next to Him would enter that same day (Luke 23:43). Two other passages that teach conscious existence after death are Jesus' parable of the unnamed rich man and Lazarus (Luke 16:19–31), who faced different circumstances after they died, and the disembodied souls of the martyred saints after their deaths (Rev. 6:9-11). However, the symbolic nature of these two texts make strict interpretations more difficult.[9]

So the resurrection of Jesus indicates that the believers will be present with Christ after their own deaths, before their bodies are raised. Later, the resurrection of their bodies will occur, also based on Jesus' resurrection (1 Thess. 1:10; 4:14). We will return to some additional aspects in the next section of this chapter.

We have already viewed Paul's teaching in 1 Corinthians 15. But it is worth the reminder that Paul rests his entire presentation of the believer's resurrection on that of Jesus, who is our Example. His resurrection has preeminence, both in importance and in time — He was the first to be raised in a new body (vv. 20-23, 47-49). The believer's resurrection follows from His (v. 12) and without it there would be no distinctly Christian hope (vv. 18–19). The conclusion of the entire matter is that final victory over death is ours through Jesus Christ (v. 57).

In Philippians 3:20-21, Paul adds an additional angle. Believers are already citizens of heaven, in contrast to those whose mind is on their earthly desires (vv. 17-19). As citizens of heaven we await Jesus' return from there to change our earthly bodies to be like His glorified body (vv. 20-21).

Raised Like Jesus

Paul addresses this subject in other places, as well. In Ephesians 2:6-7 believers are raised up with Christ to sit with Him in the heavenly realms, to learn of His grace and kindness. There is some difference between commentators as to whether Romans 6:8-9 and 8:10-11 refer to being physically or spiritually raised with Christ in order to conquer sin.[10] What might be taken as Paul's summary statement is found in 1 Corinthians 6:14: "By his power God raised the Lord from the dead, and he will raise us also."

John continues this same theme that is so frequently sounded throughout the New Testament. He teaches that there is still much that we do not know about our future state. Yet, believers can be sure that when Jesus comes for His church, they will both see Him and become like Him (1 John 3:2).

In conclusion, the New Testament presents a unified voice; the writers who comment on the subject agree that because Jesus was raised from the dead, so believers will likewise be raised. Further, Christians will have bodies like the glorious body of Jesus Himself. He is our Model. Although at death the believer may be temporarily disembodied, he is with the Lord in a far better state, awaiting the resurrection of the dead.

> Believers can be sure that when Jesus comes for His church, they will both see Him and become like Him.

JESUS' RESURRECTION AND OTHER FUTURE EVENTS

A number of New Testament texts also relate the resurrection of Jesus to future events such as the Rapture, the Second Coming, and final judgment. We will briefly address each of

Resurrection: Heart of New Testament Doctrine

these subjects, not to comment on the intricacies of the doctrines themselves, but simply to note their relationship to Jesus' being raised.

We have seen that the resurrection of believers is patterned after Jesus' resurrection. Jesus was raised almost two thousand years ago. Is there any indication when believers will experience the same? While we are not told exactly when this glorious event will occur, believers are informed that it will take place when Jesus comes for His church — the event usually called the Rapture. We will not attempt to discuss the often debated issue of the timing of the Rapture. Our point is that whenever this event occurs, believers will be raised from the dead.

Perhaps the clearest passage relating the Rapture to the resurrection of Jesus is 1 Thessalonians 4:13-18. Here Paul explains that Jesus died and rose again, and that when Jesus comes for His church, He will bring with Him those who died beforehand (v. 14). These dead believers will be the first to receive their new bodies (v. 16),[11] followed by those who are still alive (v. 17a). Then all believers will be with Christ forever (v. 17b). This teaching should bring comfort to Christians (v. 18).

The Rapture is apparently also spoken of in 1 Thessalonians 1:9-10, where, once again, we are told that Jesus died, rose again, and will return to rescue believers from God's wrath. Likewise, passages like Philippians 3:20-21 and 1 John 3:2, which also speak of Jesus' coming for believers, should best be considered as references to this same event.

It should be noted that Jewish theology emphasized the *corporate* aspect of the resurrection of the body. The righteous would rise from the dead together (Dan. 12:2; Isa. 26:19). Similarly, whenever Paul speaks of the resurrection of the dead, he does so in the plural. While individuals are resurrected and

Raised Like Jesus

each one will be recognized as himself or herself, just as Jesus was, it is viewed from its corporate scenario.

This is a major difference between Christian thought and several other views of the afterlife. The Christian view emphasizes the reality of both individual and corporate aspects. In the life to come, believers will always remain themselves. Yet, they will also share with one another in an unprecedented manner.[12]

Jesus' resurrection is also related to His Second Coming in other Scriptures. After Jesus appeared to His followers for the last time, He ascended to heaven in their presence. While they were watching Him, two men (presumably angels) suddenly stood with them. They instructed His followers that Jesus would return to earth in the same manner (Acts 1:9-11). So Jesus would return in a visible and bodily fashion. Therefore, His Second Coming will not be a strictly spiritual event. It will occur in a manner similar to His departure from the earth.

This truth is also stated in Revelation 1:7. When Jesus returns to earth the second time, everyone will see Him.[13] This passage may even infer that those who crucified Him will know it is He from His wounds, which will be visible. Jesus would then be recognized as the One who was pierced.

Jesus' resurrection is also related to judgment. Paul connects Jesus' resurrection with that of the believer (2 Cor. 4:7–5:9, especially 4:14), concluding by explaining that Christians must stand before the resurrected Christ in order to give an accounting of the things they have done (2 Cor. 5:10). Here believers receive rewards for their service after they became Christians.

> When Jesus returns to earth the second time, everyone will see Him.

On the other hand, unbelievers at Areopagus were warned

that the resurrection of Jesus ensures the truthfulness of the gospel message and judgment awaits those who refuse to repent (Acts 17:30-31). In the Book of Revelation we are told that the living Christ also holds the keys to death and Hell (Rev. 1:18). Final judgment is a reality (cf. Rev. 20:11-15).

One additional future event should also be mentioned. Paul explains that God's creation is laboring under the price tag of human sin and is therefore in bondage. However, he concludes that, just as the bodies of believers will be raised, fallen creation will also be transformed (Rom. 8:18-23). So this new creation depends on the resurrection of the body, which follows from Jesus' resurrection (Rom. 8:11).

Jesus' resurrection not only guarantees the believer's resurrection, but is also linked with other future events. The Rapture, Second Coming, and the Judgment of both believers and unbelievers are all spoken of in the context of this historical event. The transformation of God's creation is even compared to the resurrection of both Jesus and the believer. So Jesus' resurrection is a central, essential feature of eschatological doctrine, as well. The next chapter will give yet another example of this.

> Jesus' resurrection is a central, essential feature of eschatological doctrine.

APPLICATION

Once again, the resurrection of Jesus also produces a few areas of application. A couple of these can even help us to see that theology has the potential to literally change our quality of life on a day-to-day basis. The truth that believers will someday

Raised Like Jesus

live with Jesus can revolutionize the way we think and live our lives. Three areas will be mentioned here.

First, we need to briefly mention the significance of an important theological discussion. The recent dialogue among evangelicals regarding the nature of Jesus' resurrection body is not just an idle dispute.[14] It is imperative that emphasis be placed not only on the fact of Jesus' actual, physical body but also on the practical ramifications that hinge on the truthfulness of this doctrine. At the very least, we must be careful to emphasize the clear proclamation (especially in the Gospels and Acts) that the body of Jesus that was crucified and buried was the same one that was raised.[15] The staightforward teaching of the resurrection body of Jesus in the first five books of the New Testament is the chief obstacle to alternate formulations. For us to teach otherwise is to call into question a large number of biblical texts.

> The truth that believers will someday live with Jesus can revolutionize the way we think and live our lives.

Second, that believers will be raised and possess bodies like Jesus' is a final epitaph on the curse of death. There will come a day when such matters will no longer be preparatory. Hope will yield to reality, and death will finally be defeated. The resurrected Jesus will stand before us and we will instantly know that it was all worth it! As Paul proclaims:

> "Where, O death, is your victory?
>
> Where, O death, is your sting?

But God has provided the victory for us through Jesus Christ our Lord" (1 Cor. 15:51-58).

Resurrection: Heart of New Testament Doctrine

This is a subject not only for rejoicing, but also for meditation. We need to spend some quality time reflecting on the eternal blessings that have been given so freely to believers. To allow this truth to soak into us so that it really becomes a part of our deepest beliefs and longings can have a transforming effect on our lives. In our companion volume on the resurrection and Christian practice, we will address how this can take place in regard to the subject of the fear of death.

> The realization that the future resurrection of believers is as sure as the reality of Jesus' resurrection should comfort us in our grieving for departed loved ones.

Third, the realization that the future resurrection of believers is as sure as the reality of Jesus' resurrection should produce a great catalyst among Christians to be totally committed to the Lord (1 Cor. 15:58). It should also comfort us in our own grieving for departed loved ones (1 Thess. 4:17-18).[16] In short, the assurance which can come from the knowledge of the reality of the resurrection of Jesus is another benefit in this present life which should motivate believers to more fully live a consistent Christian life in all of its aspects. Jesus could actually return at any time (Matt. 24:42-51).

In fact, there are few doctrines that should have more ability to inspire the believer to act in accord with the leading of the Holy Spirit than the connection between Jesus' resurrection and the Christian's. The historical reality of the former even provides a window on the believer's future state. Ought such truth not help us to be more committed to the Lord Jesus who died, was buried, was raised, and is coming again for us? I have long thought that if Christians fully realized that our capacities to learn, grow, and serve in heaven will depend in large measure on what we have done for the Lord since our conversions to Christ, we might all be far more committed to Him.

NOTES

1. Even if we take the common view that Mark ends at 16:8, we still learn some important items about Jesus' appearances from this Gospel. In these verses, Jesus' tomb was found empty (16:4). The women were told that the same Jesus who had been crucified and buried had been raised and that the disciples would see Him in Galilee (16:6-7). It is clear, then, that Mark also teaches that the same Jesus whose body had occupied the tomb was raised and would soon appear.

2. In the King James Version, it appears as if Jesus did not allow Mary Magdelene to touch Him (John 20:17). However, the Greek actually indicates the opposite, as translated by the NASB, NIV, and other versions. Jesus told Mary to stop holding on to Him! Not only is there no problem here, but we have a further indication of Jesus' corporeality: He was being physically detained from carrying on His duties!

3. The contrast between Acts 9:7 and 22:9 regarding whether or not Paul's companions heard Jesus' voice is cleared up by the Greek if we follow versions like the NASB and NIV. The men heard Jesus' voice (9:7) but didn't understand or comprehend the meaning of the message (22:9).

4. Besides 1 Cor. 15:50, this phrase is used in Matt. 16:17, Gal. 1:16, Eph. 6:12, and Heb. 2:14. The NIV translates two of these passages (Matt. 16:17 and Gal. 1:16) simply as "man." Williams translates all four passages into their equivalent phrases: Matt. 16:17 as "man," Gal. 1:16 as "human creatures," Eph. 6:12 as "human foes," and Heb. 2:14 as "mortal nature." See Charles B. Williams, *The New Testament: In the Language of the People* (Chicago: Moody, 1966).

5. Of the available studies in this area, easily the best is Robert H. Gundry's *Soma in Biblical Theology: With Emphasis on Pauline Anthropology* (Cambridge: Cambridge University Press, 1976; Grand Rapids: Zondervan, 1987), especially Chapters 12-13.

6. Perhaps the text that is most used to argue that Jesus was created is Col. 1:15. But we have already seen that, just three verses later (Col. 1:18), the same term is used to refer to Jesus' resurrection. "Firstborn" means

"preeminent," as when King David is called "firstborn" in Ps. 89:20-27 in spite of the fact that he was the *last* of Jesse's sons to be born. Neither was he Israel's first king. But the clincher here is that the very same verse that applies this term to David explains the word: he was called the firstborn in the sense of being the most exalted (or preeminent) king on earth (Ps. 89:27). Interpreting Paul in the context, then, Jesus is preeminent over creation in the sense of being its Creator, as the apostle says in the very next verse (Col. 1:16; cf. John 1:3). See Norman L. Geisler and Ron Rhodes, *When Cultists Ask: A Popular Handbook on Cultic Misinterpretations* (Grand Rapids: Baker, 1997), pp. 259-260.

7. See especially Gundry, *Soma,* Chapter 12.

8. Williams translates this phrase: "far, far better."

9. For more on the intermediate state, see Gary R. Habermas and J.P. Moreland, *Beyond Death: Exploring the Evidence for Immortality* (Wheaton: Crossway Books, 1998), Chapter 10.

10. Of these two passages, Rom. 6:8-9 appears to be the clearer reference to believers being physically raised with Christ. We will address these passages further in the chapter "Daily Power" in *The Resurrection: Heart of the Christian Life*.

11. The contrast between 1 Thess. 4:14 and 4:16 is very instructive in terms of our earlier discussion of the believer's intermediate state after death and before the resurrection. It is possible that we also see a glimpse of this teaching here where dead believers accompany Jesus in His coming for His church (v. 14) and shortly thereafter experience the resurrection of their bodies (v. 16). That they are conscious *before* their bodies are raised may point, however briefly, to this intermediate condition.

12. A good example of the back and forth contrast between individuation and corporate sharing before death can be seen in 1 Cor. 12:12,14,20,24-27. That death does not end these relationships is seen, for example, in 1 Cor. 13:12 and Eph. 2:6-7, where there is both a knowing self and a deeper, fuller knowledge of others.

13. See also Matt. 24:27,30; Mark 13:26; and Luke 17:24; 21:27.

14. See Norman L. Geisler, *The Battle for the Resurrection* (Nashville: Thomas Nelson, 1989), and Murray Harris, *From Grave to Glory: Resurrection in the New Testament* (Grand Rapids: Zondervan, 1990).

15. Geisler is correct that "the intramural debate" among orthodox scholars as to whether *every particle* of Jesus' physical body was restored is *not* the crucial issue. This is not a necessary position for the one who holds that Jesus was raised in the same body in which He died. (See Geisler, Ibid., Appendix A.)

16. We will return to the subjects of total commitment, grief, and suffering in our companion volume, *The Resurrection: Heart of the Christian Life*.

SUGGESTED READINGS

Camp, Norman H. *The Resurrection of the Human Body.* Chicago: Moody, 1937.

Gaffin, Jr., Richard B. *Resurrection and Redemption: A Study in Paul's Soteriology.* Phillipsburg: Presbyterian and Reformed, 1978. Part Two.

Gundry, Robert H. *Soma in Biblical Theology: With Emphasis on Pauline Anthropology.* Cambridge: Cambridge University Press, 1976; Grand Rapids: Zondervan, 1987. Especially Chapter 13.

Habermas, Gary R., and J.P. Moreland, *Beyond Death: Exploring the Evidence for Immortality.* Wheaton: Crossway Books, 1998. Chapters 10, 12.

Hunt, Gladys. *Don't Be Afraid to Die: A Realistic Look at Death* (formerly titled *The Christian Way of Death*). Grand Rapids: Zondervan, 1971. Especially Chapter 3.

Miller, Laurence W. *Jesus Christ Is Alive.* Boston: W.A. Wilde, 1949. Chapter IV.

Reflecting on Lesson Five

1. Do you think there is any significance in the fact that the resurrection of Jesus is connected more frequently to the believer's resurrection (over a dozen times in the New Testament) than to any other doctrine? Why or why not?

2. Take a sheet of paper and draw a line down the middle from top to bottom. On the left side, number and list as many items as you can think of

that characterize Jesus' resurrection body. Corresponding to each one, on the right side write a "yes" or "no" according to whether that item also describes the believer's resurrection body. What have you learned about the resurrection bodies of each?

3. Without looking back over the chapter, describe in your own words as many areas as you can for holding that Jesus was raised in the same body in which He died. What is the overall importance of holding that there was bodily continuity before and after the cross?

4. How should the knowledge that the believer's resurrection is as sure as Jesus' resurrection help you to face death? We are told in Hebrews 2:14-15 that Jesus came to remove from us the fear of death. Is that even possible? How? Think of some ways this theological truth can have practical results in handling your own anxieties.

5. Why should this same knowledge also lead believers to total commitment to Jesus Christ? Do you think the hope of the resurrection provides any motivation for living the Christian life? Give some reasons for your conviction.

Consider this:

Most of us are patriotic about our country. We consider our citizenship a privilege to be cherished. Do you feel that way about your citizenship in heaven? How real to you is your present possession of eternal life? In preparing for lesson six consider the difference the view of life and death from God's perspective makes to your present reality.

6
A FORETASTE OF HEAVEN

In this lesson:
- Eternal life beginning now and extending into the future
- The reality of heaven — what we can know about it
- Responding to images of heaven

When my wife passed away in 1995 after a brief bout with cancer, I was in a dilemma concerning how best to deal with the emotional needs of our four children, all of whom were living at home. Often they needed an emotional "quick fix" to feel better. During those times, I resorted most frequently to repeating a truth that seemed to be very helpful. It was something that also worked years earlier when their grandfather had passed away.

88   **A Foretaste of Heaven**

"Mom wouldn't come back from heaven, even if she could," I would tell them. This, more than anything else, seemed to have a calming effect. If necessary, I would add other snippets: "Heaven is so beautiful. She is there with Grandpa and Grandma. She cares about us very much, and she knows we'll be all right, too."

I believe these truths deeply, as well. They not only helped our children, but they brought much comfort to me, too, whenever I mentioned them.[1]

What is the basis for this hope? Is heaven worth the wait? Will it be everything we hope it will? A chapter that links Jesus' resurrection to the reality of heaven is a fitting conclusion to the first of our two volumes. Here we join the supreme historical fact of the past with the greatest future reality. What a fantastic combination! In between these two doctrinal bookends, the New Testament repeatedly encourages believers to apply the truth of each to their earthly lives in order to live more profitably.

JESUS' RESURRECTION AND HEAVEN

In our last chapter we indicated that there is a strong correlation between the resurrection of Jesus and the future resurrection of believers. We will have bodies that are patterned after Jesus' glorious body (Phil. 3:21). Now we can complete this picture by exploring the relationship between this fantastic historical event and the believer's heavenly home — the final consummation towards which the resurrection has pointed all along. A number of New Testament texts make this connection.

We have seen that while Jesus was on the earth, He predicted His death and resurrection on numerous occasions. He warned His disciples that He would be departing soon (John 14:28–30). He also promised that, after He had returned to heav-

A Foretaste of Heaven

en, He would prepare a place for His followers, later taking them back to be with Him there (14:1-4).

For Paul, the process from salvation to sanctification to glorification is supernaturally achieved in the believer (Eph. 2:1-10). God saved us from our native, sinful state (vv. 1-5), raising us up with Jesus Christ and making us newly alive, placing us in heavenly realms with Him (vv. 5-7). As a result of our salvation, we should produce good works (vv. 8-10). Jesus' resurrection plays a key role in this process.

In some ways, this passage is reminiscent of Romans 8:28-39. After addressing the weighty theological topics of the foreknowledge, predestination, calling, justification, and glorification of Christians (vv. 28-30), Paul attempts to spell out some of the benefits that are made available to believers. Here he argues from Jesus' death and resurrection to the believer's salvation and steadfastness in the love of Jesus Christ (vv. 31-39). There is a relentless movement from salvation to glorification all made possible by the gospel facts of the death and resurrection of Jesus Christ.

But this is not just some dry survey of theology, either. Paul asks about the wonderful truth that since God loved us so much that He did not even spare His own Son, why wouldn't He give us anything else that we needed (v. 32)? Think of it! Why would He withhold anything that was truly necessary, given that He has already sacrificed His Son for us? Then, by excluding every possible enemy, Paul takes pains to

> Why would God withhold anything that was truly necessary, given that He has already sacrificed His Son for us?

point out that believers cannot be separated from God's love in

Jesus Christ (vv. 35-39). God's unparalleled love takes us all the way from salvation to eternity! Here's another fantastic comfort!

In a very picturesque scene, Revelation 5 portrays believers in heaven singing praises to the Lamb who had been dead but was now alive (vv. 6,9,12-14). His sacrifice made it possible for individuals to be there in heaven with Him (vv. 9-10).

But Christians don't have to wait until they actually arrive in heaven for some of these blessings. For the believer, eternal life begins now (John 5:24; 6:47) precisely because Jesus is Himself the resurrection and the life (John 11:25-26). Christians can know that we presently have the blessings of eternal life (1 John 5:13).

Looking at this truth from a different angle, Paul teaches that Christians are actually citizens of heaven even while living here in the present. Earth is not our true home. And it is from heaven that the risen Jesus will come and give us our eternal bodies (Phil. 3:20-21).[2] Here we have a direct line from Jesus' resurrection to the believer's heavenly abode.

> Paul teaches that Christians are actually citizens of heaven even while living here in the present.

So this grand historical event is more than a guarantee of our future existence in heaven, as fantastic as that will be one day. This occurrence also provides meaning in our everyday Christian lives. In the passage just mentioned (Phil. 3:20-21), it is the believer's heavenly citizenship and hope of resurrection that furnishes the necessary motivation not to live for physical desires. Paul tells us that this is a worthy antidote to earthly cravings like feeding our stomachs and seeking our own glory (vv. 17-19).

This same theme is likewise sounded in other passages that link the resurrection to the Christian's heavenly hope. In the extended text in 2 Corinthians 4:7–5:10 we have already seen that Paul addresses the subjects of persecution, suffering, and death. Basing his advice on the fact that God will raise believers from the dead the same way He raised Jesus (4:14), the apostle advises believers not to look at their troubles but at the resulting eternal life (4:16-18). We are assured of being alive with Jesus even after death (5:1-9). Paul undoubtedly thought that believers need an eternal outlook on life.

Jesus' resurrection is a pivotal truth in what I have termed the "top-down" perspective, which teaches us to look at everything in life, from our positive interests and little bothers all the way to our most severe problems, from the standpoint of God and His eternal Kingdom. Our focus should always be on God and the blessings of the eternal dimension. This is the angle from which we are repeatedly told to view our lives, including both victories and problems, providing the proper basis for our decisions. By obeying this biblical teaching, we can reorient our thinking, thereby providing the proper basis for conquering our daily anxieties, as well as even lessening the pain that so often enters our path.

> Our focus should always be on God and the blessings of the eternal dimension.

Another text that presents similar advice is 1 Peter 1:3-9. Jesus' resurrection guarantees the reality of our salvation in heaven (vv. 3-5). This truth should actually cause believers to rejoice even though they were, at that very time, suffering persecution for the cause of Christ (vv. 6-9)! So Peter thought that focusing on heaven could actually provide help against life-threatening problems in the real world!

Imagine such teachings — that our heavenly hope brought about by the knowledge that Jesus has truly been raised from the

92 A Foretaste of Heaven

dead could even be exercised in such a way that Christians could actually rejoice in the face of deadly persecution! If this was possible for them, then what does it say to us concerning refocusing our priorities in order to conquer the less severe problems that we face every day? We will return to this subject later.

So Jesus' resurrection is repeatedly placed in the context of teachings concerning heaven. This event not only indicates the reality of eternal life itself, but is also used to encourage believers to view life and its problems from God's eternal perspective. As a result, we have the motivation to live above our daily struggles.

OUR HEAVENLY HOPE

What does Jesus' resurrection actually tell us concerning the nature of heaven? We will take a look at what awaits believers in heaven by viewing *only* those aspects that are evident through either the nature of Jesus' resurrection itself or in those passages that link this event to the believer's heavenly hope.[3] The subject of heaven is certainly much broader than this, but we want to stay within the focus of this volume's theme by attempting to learn what can be known of heaven strictly from its relation to the resurrection. So we will list several features of eternal life by examining ideas that we have already presented.

(1) Heaven is a real place, not some illusory "pie in the sky in the sweet by and by." It is not just some childhood tale or fantasy, like floating in the air or sitting on imaginary clouds and playing nonexistent harps. We know this because of the reality of Jesus' resurrection appearances, which we have said were actually the initial unveiling of eternal life. Jesus' very real resurrection shows there is an actual heaven. Jesus also ascended to heaven, was glorified, and acts as our High Priest and Mediator

even now. Heaven is already in existence, as well as being the believer's future home.

(2) What is real is not necessarily substantial, but heaven is a substantial place. It is not simply a psychological reality, a state of mind, or a place for departed spirits. This is especially shown by Jesus' resurrection appearances, which were bodily in nature. Jesus was seen, touched, and heard. He ate food, walked around, and taught. Even so, heaven is an actual place for real resurrected bodies.

(3) Besides being both real and substantial, the life of heaven is eternal life. Heaven is no mere utopia where people are happy but continue to age and die. Believers experience the life that God has granted us by grace (eternal life), as well as not dying but living forever (immortality). This is a double blessing of both quality and quantity. Our lives will no longer know pain, sorrow, or death (Rev. 21:4). Additionally, believers will never die (John 11:25-26; 1 Cor. 15:51-54). In this sense, believers will be like Jesus Himself (John 14:19); they will live eternally (2 Cor. 5:1; 1 Thess. 4:17). What awesome promises! To experience heaven is to enjoy the good life forever (Ps. 16:11).

> What is real is not necessarily substantial, but heaven is a substantial place.

(4) A related thought is that our heavenly inheritance "can never perish, spoil or fade" (1 Pet. 1:4). Peter's choice of Greek terms to describe heaven's qualities indicates that our blessings are incorruptible and indestructible (*aphtharton* — a form of "immortal"), without flaw or blemish (*amianton*), and without losing its glory (*amaranton*). Further, Peter states that these blessings are "kept" or "reserved" for believers, using a term

(*teteremenen*) that indicates they are being guarded for us. This last point is reminiscent of a comment made by Paul (2 Tim. 1:12). The result is that the characteristics, nature, and blessings of heaven will not be taken away from believers or otherwise be corrupted. Our eternal inheritance is kept for us by the grace and power of God. It could not be more secure!

> Our eternal inheritance is kept for us by the grace and power of God. It could not be more secure!

(5) Believers will not only see their Lord Jesus face to face (1 John 3:2; Rev. 22:4), but will spend eternity with Him, both in the intermediate state (2 Cor. 5:8) and in heaven itself (John 14:2-3). To behold Him at last will be glorious, indeed!

(6) Beyond this, believers will be raised with Jesus, seated, and exalted with Him in heaven (Eph. 2:6). His resurrection is part of the ultimate salvific plan of God that culminates in the glorification of the saints (see Rom. 8:11,17-18,30,34).

(7) Beyond our glorification, those who have been united with Jesus in His death and resurrection (Rom. 6:4-8) will experience another blessing. We who died with Jesus will also live and reign with Him (2 Tim. 2:11-12; Rev. 5:9-10). This implies that believers will be given positions of honor and authority in God's Kingdom.

(8) Another heavenly occupation involves serving God as priests. This is proclaimed before the risen Christ by His saints (Rev. 5:10). We are not told much about what this will involve. But like worship, I'm convinced that it will be an activity that will not only be directed toward God, but will be a wonderful blessing for us.

(9) Believers will also be given the opportunity to join in praising both Jesus Christ, the slain but living Lamb of God, and His Father (Rev. 5:6,9-10,12-14). This promises to be the largest choir

A Foretaste of Heaven 95

ever assembled for a spontaneous time of singing praise that simply flows out of hearts full of gratitude to God. These will be the ultimate times of worship; we will be roused beyond anything we've ever experienced before! This will be one of the supreme fulfillments of our longing for God.

(10) Another grand blessing of heaven involves the collective aspect. Besides passages apart from the context of Jesus' resurrection that indicate the fellowship that believers will share with each other (see Matt. 8:11; 1 Cor. 13:12; Rev. 21:26-27), we need to remember that the resurrection of the dead is corporate in nature. We have said that Paul always speaks of it in the plural. In fact, in Romans 1:3-4, Paul even speaks of Jesus' resurrection in the plural, as if to include the future of believers with Him, as well. Both dead and living believers will be raised together and will share in this glorious occasion (1 Thess. 4:14-18). We will be reunited with our loved ones who have died in Christ before us. We will all join together in praising the resurrected Christ (Rev. 5:9-14).

(11) Another of the most exciting aspects of heavenly life is that we will apparently continue to grow spiritually by increasing in our knowledge of God's grace. Paul says that we will know one another to an even greater extent than we do now (1 Cor. 13:12). The apostle also tells us that, after being raised with Christ, we will be shown "the incomparable riches of his grace" through-

> If God is revealing more of Himself, we will continue to learn!

out the coming ages. If God is revealing more of Himself, we will continue to learn! Further, such a conclusion can also be drawn from our very nature as finite human beings. Even after our own resurrection, we will still be glorified human persons, not omniscient beings. And although we will no longer be mortal, it is our very nature to learn as we live.

96 A Foretaste of Heaven

(12) Furthermore, just as the bodies of believers are redeemed, raised, and glorified, so fallen creation itself will be "redeemed," becoming God's new creation (Rom. 8:19-23). Being freed from decay and reaching its glorious potential (8:21), only righteousness will dwell in the new earth (2 Pet. 3:13; Rev. 21:1). This is the world in which believers will live as well as enjoy — God's paradise (Rev. 2:7), which encourages visions of the Garden of Eden (Gen. 2:8).

(13) Lastly, the believer's citizenship in heaven, with its eternal life, can even begin now. We don't have to wait until we die to secure some of the blessings of such life! It begins after redemption for the believer, including the power to avoid sin, conquer the fear of death, and experience the greatest motivation in the world, one that looks forward to eternity with God and our saved loved ones.[4] What incomparable blessings! These blessings are directly due to the resurrection of Jesus (John 11:25-26; Phil. 3:20-21).

Heaven is truly a glorious place. While we are told numerous truths that heighten our expectations, there is also much that we do *not* presently know about it (1 Cor. 2:9; 13:12; 1 John 3:2). So we can adopt a kind of "Christmas morning" view of heaven that allows us to anticipate its glories and blessings. Believers know enough, though, to look forward to an incomparable time of fellowship with Jesus Christ Himself and with our Christian loved ones. I often wonder what the all-powerful God of the universe could have planned for us from before the world was created (Matt. 25:34)!

APPLICATION

A chapter on heaven allows us to bring together many details concerning a subject that we have viewed from several different

A Foretaste of Heaven

angles in these two volumes on the centrality of Jesus' resurrection. It is difficult to exhaust this topic or grow tired of hearing about it. It is God's gift to His followers. We ought to take much joy in it. Some of our thoughts for application build on our other discussions. Others launch us into new directions for us to consider in the light of heaven.

First, we said in Chapter 4 that the resurrection of Jesus provides a strong, twofold confirmation of eternal life, both indirect and direct. Indirectly, God validated Jesus' teachings by raising Him from the dead (Chapter 3). Therefore, since the Kingdom of God, and its entrance requirements of eternal life, was Jesus' central message, it would be verified most of all. In short, if any of Jesus' themes were validated by the resurrection, heaven was, since it was His central teaching. God would not raise a heretic from the dead.

> If any of Jesus' themes were validated by the resurrection, heaven was.

Directly, the resurrection of Jesus is an actual example of eternal life. To say that Jesus was raised from the dead and appeared afterwards is to say that heaven broke into time and space for forty days. In other words, when His followers saw Him, they witnessed the presence of eternal life standing directly in front of their eyes. When they touched Him, their fingertips felt heaven. This cannot be said of any of Jesus' other miracles. But when He appeared to them, they knew heaven was a reality.

Since Jesus' central message concerned the road to eternal life, this teaching was verified by His resurrection. Such an evidential basis is important, for it reveals the truthfulness of this important teaching.

So why are we reviewing this here? Having spent this chapter on the reality of heaven, we have prepared ourselves to view life

A Foretaste of Heaven

from God's eternal perspective. Heaven is the crowning gift of God's grace to us. Seen from the theoretical angle, it is established both indirectly and directly by the incredible event of Jesus' resurrection. Viewed practically, we are inspired by its reality and its ability to meet all of our needs. The combination of theory and practice is unbeatable!

> Heaven is the crowning gift of God's grace to us.

Second, in this chapter we only viewed the connection between Jesus' resurrection and heaven. But there is much more to the subject than this. Scripture indicates other exciting prospects about heaven as well, still without coming near to being exhaustive. One angle that deserves addressing is what J.P. Moreland and I call the imagery of heaven. Some of the most incredible things we learn about this place are what Scripture doesn't tell us!

Humans seem to share deep-seated desires for certain immensely powerful concepts like beauty, peace, rest, protection, security, and intimate fellowship. Sometimes we want these things in a temporal sort of way — after a long day of work or when vacation comes. But it seems that many of us also associate these items with eternity — they are among the things we would like to spend our time experiencing forever. Either way, we often cannot put these desires into words or quantify them with descriptions.

Scripture relates each of these ideas to both temporal and eternal settings. Some examples are not difficult to produce. The pristine Garden of Eden (Gen. 2:8-15) and the magnificence of God's New Jerusalem are both called paradise (cf. Gen. 2:8 with Rev. 2:7). Both are symbols of beauty for believers. Who is not blessed by the peaceful imagery of the Good Shepherd in Psalm

A Foretaste of Heaven

23:1-3, who leads His sheep to green pastures and quiet waters? This same theme is picked up in Revelation 7:15-17, with Jesus leading His sheep beside springs of living water. Likewise, God granted rest to the Jews (Ps. 81:6-7), just as Jesus offered it to His hearers (Matt. 11:29). Rest is also promised to those who die for the Lord (Rev. 14:13).

> Who is not blessed by the peaceful imagery of the Good Shepherd in Psalm 23:1-3, who leads His sheep to green pastures and quiet waters?

Another deep image is that of God's protection, with His people hidden under the shadow of His wings or within His mighty fortress (Ps. 91:1-4). Similarly, God's ultimate fortress is specially created for believers for all eternity (Rev. 21). The Old Testament idea of fellowship often involved a feast (Zech. 14:16). Jesus also promised that believers would come from all over the world to enjoy a feast together in God's Kingdom (Matt. 8:11-12), of which the greatest may be the marriage supper of the Lamb (Rev. 19:7-9). The best fellowship of all will be seeing our Lord face to face (Rev. 22:4).

True, it is very difficult to determine which images are to be taken literally and which ones are not. But that's exactly the point! The Holy Spirit gets the message across precisely by allowing us to dream, to picture God's delicious gifts for His loved ones. His images bring smiles to our faces and sighs to our lips! They hit us right in the heart! It might even be said that the imagery of heaven gives us freedom to wish, perhaps providing greater blessings than straightforward prose could ever do.[5] Francis Schaeffer once said that, "The Christian is the one whose imagination should fly beyond the stars."[6] Yes, the believers' imaginations should lead them all the way to eternity!

Third, we have made some comments about a "top-down" perspective that views the various aspects of our lives from God's eternal standpoint. Scripture encourages us to adopt such a perspective on life as a whole. More specifically, we are told to apply this remedy to situations such as anxiety, persecution, suffering, loving others, our physical needs, even death, as well as to our finances. Each of these areas needs a strong dose of heaven. A good summary text is Col. 3:2: "Set your minds on things above, not on earthly things."

In each of these instances, the "top floor" remains the same, consisting of God and His Kingdom. The "bottom floor" changes regularly, depending on the items that occupy our lives, like those we just listed. The chief idea is to formulate outlooks and behaviors in every area of our lives (with our families, other relationships, jobs, and ministries) according to how they are informed by the upper floor. As Jesus told us, what we treasure will determine our heart's focus (Matt. 6:21). If our desires are centered on God and His Kingdom (6:19-20,33), we can develop a mentality that views everything through an eternal filter. The result is something we all need — a simpler life that grows less and less complicated because we are single-minded in our goals and perspective.

Questions to ask ourselves about a certain subject or problem include some of these: How does the holiness of God shed light on this issue? Do we really desire Him for who He is? How can our own pursuit of spirituality and holiness assist us in facing these concerns? Does a single-minded quest for heaven change the perspective on the earthly subject? What difference will our problem make 1,000 years from now? Streamlining our lives with an eye toward eternity sheds an entirely new light on earth.

Scripture exhorts us to constantly implement these new thinking patterns (see Phil. 4:6-9).[7] We need to replace our misbeliefs and nonbiblical loyalties with biblical truths. Perhaps our target on the lower level is our materialistic mind-set, constant worries, or a lack of motivation to follow God. In its place, we need a heavenly perspective to inspire us to action and change. What could be more motivational than experiencing eternity with the God of creation and our believing loved ones? Then our lives should major on matters pertaining to this first love and let other things that don't fit the biblical, eternal perspective fall by the wayside. After all, it is usually these other elements that cause most of our pain and unrest anyway.

> We need to replace our misbeliefs and nonbiblical loyalties with biblical truths.

One key here is the realization that God and His desires for us are not something that we should resent, as if they were some new law. God wants to fulfill our deepest desires — a meaningful and fulfilling life here that lasts forever. We should prefer God's ways over our own. After all, death is the greatest evil in life. Living the good life is arguably the greatest good. If this is so, then living the good life forever is the best possible offer. These New Testament texts do not just promote a problem-solving technique by itself, as useful as that is, but an entire lifestyle. Its results are revolutionary.[8]

Fourth, this discussion brings up the question concerning the place of rewards. If believers truly understood that heavenly blessings are based on one's stewardship after salvation,[9] God's offer might have a far more important place in influencing our actions.

Of course, this also raises questions, too. What are our motives for seeking rewards? Is it possible that we desire them for their own sake or for the glory that they may bring us? Clearly,

102 **A Foretaste of Heaven**

these would not be biblical reasons. On the other hand, God has placed within us the desire for eternal fellowship with Him, our loved ones, and other believers. So He has provided a biblical motivation. In addition, He has even instructed Christians to seek heavenly rewards![10]

Therefore, the pursuit of rewards is not necessarily mistaken, since God provides our internal desire, as well as charging us to pursue the treasures. This is especially the case when we study the nature of these rewards. Instead of items for the purpose of showing off, they may possibly be some sort of capacity for greater service, growth, learning, and fellowship. Thus, they may actually increase our abilities to do the sorts of things that God encourages us to do. So the question of motivation becomes a major one. There is a selfish, proud way to seek them, too, but this is not God's way.

Peter Kreeft proposes a thought experiment in order to assist believers in determining these motives. What would we say if God offered us whatever we most wanted in life? What would we take if, whatever it was, it was ours for the asking? Would it be wealth? Power? Honor? How about peace of mind? But while you are thinking it over, God goes on to explain that there is only one thing you may not choose. You will never see His face.

What would our response be to this declaration? Would you be secretly satisfied to take one of the many other treasures, or would you be emotionally crushed by the last condition? Where do your true desires lie? Do you desire God and His Kingdom above all else? Such an experiment might help to provide an answer to the question of our secret desires and our ultimate motivation.[11]

Fifth, eternal life in heaven is the final remedy to death. And it is the fulfillment of our deepest longings. We've been leading up to this answer through this entire book. Did you ever have an intense desire to study and learn more about God and His universe? Have you ever been stirred beyond words in a praise service, as if you couldn't even stand the joy? Have you enjoyed a night or a vacation so full of fellowship with others that you never wanted to leave? Have you ever been moved by a few moments alone in God's nature — perhaps in a beautiful garden, or near a thundering waterfall, snow-topped mountains, or a quiet lake in the middle of the woods? Heaven is beyond our wildest dreams, and it has been promised to those who are in love with Jesus Christ!

> Heaven is beyond our wildest dreams, and it has been promised to those who are in love with Jesus Christ!

In eternity, the most widespread fear known to humans is behind us; it is over, finished. Heaven is the final epitaph on pain, suffering, sin, and death (Rev. 21:4). They will no longer raise their ugly heads again; their reign is over. As C.S. Lewis ends his last Narnian chronicle, "they were beginning Chapter One of the Great Story, which no one on earth has read: which goes on for ever: in which every chapter is better than the one before."[12] Indeed, God is the ultimate Victor — eternal life wins out over the grave! Jesus' resurrection is God's trump card on evil and death!

NOTES

1. Our family's story is told in Gary R. Habermas, *Forever Loved: A Personal Account of Grief and Resurrection* (Joplin, MO: College Press, 1997).

2. This idea is reminiscent of a similar theme concerning the believers who, throughout this life, were actually strangers on earth looking forward to their heavenly home (Heb. 11:8-10,13-16,24-27).

3. It should be carefully noted that when we speak about the heavenly "hope," as Peter does in 1 Pet. 1:3, we are not subjecting the Christian's beliefs about heaven to a mere "hope so" mentality. This is not the meaning of the New Testament term. In fact, in this context, Peter bases this hope on the fact of the resurrection. The hope of heaven is as sure as is this historical event!

4. These and other subjects are the focus of volume II, *The Resurrection: Heart of the Christian Life*.

5. For a development of the imagery of heaven, see Habermas and Moreland, *Beyond Death*, Chapter 13, pp. 272-276.

6. Francis Schaeffer, *Art and the Bible* (Downers Grove, IL: InterVarsity, 1973), p. 61.

7. In our second volume, this strategy is explained in detail and serves as our chief method for application to both emotional and volitional doubt. We will also argue that this is a powerful tool in dealing with and overcoming sin, not by striving in our own strength, but in the resurrection power provided by the Holy Spirit.

8. More details, including the principle itself and some practical ways in which to apply it, may be found elsewhere. See Gary R. Habermas, *Dealing with Doubt* (Chicago: Moody, 1990), Chapter 9; Habermas and Moreland, *Beyond Death*, Chapter 15; Gary R. Habermas, "Top Down Thinking and the Problems on Earth," *Christian Counseling Today*, Vol. 6, No. 2 (1998), pp. 26-28, 66-67.

9. By stewardship, I do not simply refer to what we do with our finances, although this is very important. Rather, I am thinking of our total individual response to the Lord with the means He has provided for us and allowed us to develop. Besides the gifts that we give back to the Lord, how do we spend our time? How do we use the spiritual gifts that He has given us? These are some of the questions that each believer needs to answer in personal terms.

10. See Matt 6:19-21; Luke 12:32-34; 14:13-14; I Tim. 6:17-19. While referring particularly to eternal life itself, texts like Luke 16:9 and Gal. 6:8-10 may also include rewards.

11. Peter Kreeft, *Heaven: The Heart's Deepest Longing* (San Francisco: Harper and Row, 1980), p. 27.

12. C.S. Lewis, *The Last Battle* (New York: Collier Books, 1956), p. 184.

SUGGESTED READINGS

Habermas, Gary R. *The Resurrection of Jesus: An Apologetic.* Grand Rapids: Baker, 1980; Lanham: University Press of America, 1984. Chapters 4-5.

Habermas, Gary R., and J.P. Moreland. *Beyond Death: Exploring the Evidence for Immortality.* Wheaton: Crossway Books, 1998. Chapters 12–15.

Harris, Murray J. "Resurrection and Immortality in the Pauline Corpus." In *Life in the Face of Death: The Resurrection Message of the New Testament.* Ed. by Richard N. Longenecker. Grand Rapids: Eerdmans, 1998.

MacArthur, Jack. *Exploring in the Next World.* Minneapolis: Bethany Fellowship, 1967.

Reflecting on Lesson Six

1. For group discussion: Imagine yourself trying to comfort children who had just lost a parent. If they wanted to talk through some of their grief, what would you share with them? After losing three sons, Joseph Bayly advised the following, especially when speaking to children about the subject: "I believe that our teaching about death should be coupled with teaching about heaven, that the emphasis should be on transition rather than cessation." (Joseph Bayly, *The View from a Hearse* [Elgin: Cook Publishing, 1969], p. 46.) Does this provide some helpful directions for your thoughts and comments? Which truths about heaven do you think would be the most helpful to share?

2. What else does Jesus' resurrection tell us about heaven? Include references along with your responses.

3. When Paul tells us that we are citizens of heaven (Phil. 3:20-21), what do you think he had in mind? How is a similar idea developed in Hebrews 11:13-16? What are some of the benefits that a citizen might have? What does this say about our life on earth?

106 **A Foretaste of Heaven**

4. For group discussion: Evaluate the point in the Application section regarding the imagery of heaven. How do you describe the force that these word pictures have on you? Do you recognize any inaudible sighs deep in your soul? Do they awaken any longings? How do you explain your reaction (or lack of one)?

5. For group discussion: Let each person name a problem or concern from everyday life. Then, together, consider several ways that issue might be handled from God's heavenly viewpoint. How might the light of heaven illumine the topic? In each instance, state some *specific* steps that might address the problem.

6. Do you agree with the answer given here regarding heavenly rewards? What do you think they are? What does Scripture mean by commanding believers to pursue them? Must this always be a selfish quest?

Consider this:

In the multicultural environment of our world today the Christian is presented with many different kinds of challenges to the unique claims of Christianity. Before looking at Lesson Seven think about one or two of these different approaches (e.g., New Age, atheism, Hinduism, Islam, etc.) and determine how you could use the resurrection of Jesus to show someone the truth of Christianity and its claims.

7

THE CENTER OF NEW TESTAMENT THEOLOGY

In this lesson:
- ▶ The centrality of Christ's resurrection reiterated
- ▶ Looking at the many facets of this gospel truth
- ▶ Responding to non-Christian views

Have you ever taken a really close look at an expensive diamond? Were you surprised by the cut and clarity of the stone while viewing it under a magnifying glass? The overall beauty can be stunning. When turned one way the light strikes certain facets and takes on distinct shapes. When turned in another direction, it seems to take on an entirely new look. It is almost as if there is a whole world strangely present before your eyes, all within the stone.

108 The Center of New Testament Theology

We started this volume by comparing the resurrection of Jesus to the many angles of the diamond. And we'll return to this analogy below. This event is not only the very heart of the New Testament proclamation, a point generally recognized today by scholars of widely differing theological beliefs. But this occurrence also has many angles. Our emphasis throughout has been to show that this is the case—the resurrection can be linked to a broad range of our cherished Christian doctrines. The best way to support this stance is to show just how this event is used in the New Testament.

THE CENTRAL FOCUS

In Christian publications, Jesus' resurrection is most frequently categorized either as one of the indispensable historical facts of the gospel or as the major evidence on behalf of Christianity. While these are surely its chief uses in the New Testament, we have seen that its theological importance extends far beyond both soteriology and apologetics. The resurrection of Jesus is linked to many of the major doctrines in the New Testament.

In addition to its role at the heart of the gospel and in establishing the truth of Jesus' Person and teachings, the resurrection is also coupled with topics like Jesus as our High Priest, the Rapture, Second Coming, and judgment. Its frequent connection to the resurrection of believers, as well as to the trans-

> The frequent connection of Jesus' resurrection to that of believers, as well as to the transformation of God's creation, and its foreshadowing of life in heaven are among the most blessed comparisons.

The Center of New Testament Theology

formation of God's creation, and its foreshadowing of life in heaven are among the most blessed comparisons.[1]

The single passage that best illustrates the widest variety of topics being tied to the resurrection is 1 Corinthians 15. There is a reason that it is often called the "resurrection chapter." Here, Paul begins by addressing the factual content of the gospel and the necessity of faith (vv. 1-5), followed by the eyewitness evidence for Jesus' appearances (vv. 5-11). Turning to the relationship between the resurrection and the Christian faith in verses 12-23, he links this event to the truth of Christian preaching (vv. 12-15), the resurrection of believers (vv. 12-13,15-16,17,20-23), the truth of Christianity (vv. 14,17), the forgiveness of sins (v. 17b), as well as our Christian hope (v. 19).

Paul continues with a brief discussion of certain eschatological matters (vv. 24-28), Christian ethics (vv. 29-34), the resurrection of the believer's body and immortality (vv. 35-57), finishing up with the need for total commitment to God (v. 58). In light of this passage, it would be incredible to argue that Paul was only concerned with one or two aspects of this event!

Seen from this wider perspective, the resurrection of Jesus is not an isolated event at all. It forms a single unit with the other facts of the gospel and, in turn, with the entire New Testament proclamation. This is especially the case when we move on to practical matters of spirituality in the next volume and see that it is of preeminent importance there, too. For a very simple illustration, if Jesus had not died, He could not have been raised from the dead; if He was not raised, we would not be raised like Him, either; then heaven would not be what is pictured in Scripture. Further, spirituality that is based on His teachings is also misplaced. Apart from Jesus there would be religion, but there would be no Christianity.

All of these doctrines are intricately related to one another. Further, the rest of Christian theology and practice are similarly linked to this majestic occurrence. We've just begun to get a vision for how the resurrection is interwoven with biblical truth.

The resurrection is mentioned or implied dozens of times in the New Testament in over 300 verses, in both extended and abbreviated contexts. No book longer than five chapters fails to mention it. Of the seven books that do not report it directly, four are only one chapter long and are concerned with a very narrow focus.[2] Several of these still make statements that imply the resurrection.[3] Further, five of these seven books are traditionally believed to have been written by authors who elsewhere clearly address the subject multiple times.[4]

So even though the resurrection is not mentioned in every single New Testament book, it is still the chief proclamation of the whole. When viewed as a unit along with the death and Deity of Jesus Christ, it composes the gospel, constituting the basis for our salvation. We have viewed numerous passages that make this event the foundation for Christianity. First Corinthians 15 by itself shows this centrality for Paul, since the entire Christian faith stands or falls with the resurrection of Jesus (15:14,17). For John, it is the central miracle that should lead to faith, which is the reason he wrote his Gospel (20:30-31). Matthew calls it Jesus' chief sign even for those who refuse to believe (Matt. 12:38-40; 16:1-4). Luke links it to the proclamation of Jesus' chief message: the

The Center of New Testament Theology

Kingdom of God (Acts 1:3). Peter states that the resurrection is the basis for our eternal hope in heaven, making exceptionally difficult times bearable (1 Pet. 1:3-7).

A MANY-FACETED DIAMOND

Our diamond analogy has been used in a few places in this book to illustrate the many faces of the resurrection. Just as this beautiful gemstone has many facets and can reflect light from different angles, so this historical event also has many sides. It cannot be fully explained under single labels like soteriology or apologetics. It is a very broad topic, largely because it intersects with so many other crucial areas of the Christian faith.

But let's turn the resurrection to another of its facets and look at it from still another angle. While it encompasses many themes in Christianity, we can also zero in on just one of those aspects and follow it deeply. In other words, instead of trying to give the broad picture, as we have in this book, we could

> While the resurrection encompasses many themes in Christianity, we can also zero in on just one of those aspects and follow it deeply.

zoom in on particular themes. This is something that we have not done here, but which still deserves a comment.

For example, in traditional apologetics the resurrection is often defended with the assumption that the challenger denies the supernatural realm altogether, objecting to any belief in miracles. So the Christian might argue for the possibility of miracles in general, state and defend positive arguments for the resurrection, offer objections to alternative hypotheses, or address the textual questions in the relevant biblical passages.

An interesting aspect of such a conversation is an implicit recognition on the part of both believers and unbelievers alike. Namely, both sides often recognize that if Jesus was actually raised from the dead, this would be exceptionally significant, especially because of Who Jesus claimed to be. So such an outcome would strongly favor Christian Theism.

But what if the entire scenario changed? Given recent mindsets such as that commonly represented as the "New Age Movement," an unbeliever might grant that the resurrection of Jesus actually occurred, believing that the history of religion is full of all kinds of strange and wonderful occurrences. However, while admitting the resurrection, such an individual might not be willing to recognize that anything unique follows from such an admission, precisely because these strange phenomena in the world's religions supposedly indicate that all religions are ways to God. How should the Christian proceed?

I would suggest that here we turn the resurrection in order to expose another of its many facets. While apologetic strategies can change, even in New Testament times the gospel content remained the same.[5] So it is in this case, as well. If the resurrection is granted, then work needs to be done on the uniqueness of Jesus and His claims. Here the key is to show that, if the resurrection occurred, this indeed *does* say something unique about Jesus.

> If the resurrection occurred, this indeed *does* say something unique about Jesus.

Jesus made unique claims concerning His person and message. In particular, He proclaimed that He was Deity and the only way to God. To show this would now be significant, since it would thereby be confirmed by His resurrection (see Chapter 3).

The Center of New Testament Theology 113

In contrast, other founders of world religions *did not* make these same sorts of claims that Jesus did.[6] Since Jesus' teachings are proven by His resurrection, He is unique and all religions *cannot* represent valid ways to God.[7] Another worthwhile method is to challenge the non-Christian's supernatural claims on their own grounds — how do we know that there are parallels in other religions?[8]

This is simply a brief example of how two facets of the resurrection might work. This event verifies Jesus' unique teachings. If the resurrection is challenged, we need to display the strong arsenal of evidences in its favor. If His distinctive teachings are challenged, we turn this gem another way. Appropriate steps then need to be taken to show that Jesus did make these claims. But the basic gospel content never changes. A different aspect of the resurrection is showcased on each occasion.

No other biblical miracle can claim to have these multiple functions, the amount of evidence, or the important applications of the resurrection message. Changing the water to wine or feeding the 5,000 were wonderful occurrences, but they do not necessarily prove the Deity of Christ or indicate the truthfulness of the believer's resurrection from the dead, at least like Jesus' resurrection does. At once, this grand event provides evidence for (and is otherwise related to) most of the fundamental doctrines of Christianity, such as revealing God's creative powers. In the resurrection we even move a step beyond the initial creation: the power of God's *new* creation is evident, manifest in Jesus' immortal resurrection body, signifying the dawn of God's eternal Kingdom.

> The basic gospel content never changes; a different aspect of the resurrection is showcased on each occasion.

Another theological perspective from which to view this event is that it signals a mighty act of God's nature and grace. What knowledge and power He must have to even perform such a miracle! Modern science cannot begin to fathom such an occurrence, let alone doing so in a glorified body. And what grace that brought together such a multitude of apologetic, theological, and practical truths in one event! What if this amount of evidence were available for some other miracle but not for the resurrection? The overall case for Christianity would be much less than it is now.

In other words, God's power is obviously manifest in the resurrection, but so is His grace. Such a convergence of power, evidence, and ultimate meaning in one event, not to mention its complementary nature with regard to evidencing and completing other doctrines, is a masterpiece of divine design. Such an occurrence provides incredible insights into God's grace, especially since it was performed on the behalf of His beloved. We are told that, throughout the ages to come, we will continue to witness divine grace through Jesus Christ (Eph. 2:7). Believers need to meditate deeply on these truths.

> Such a convergence is a masterpiece of divine design.

Here is but a glimpse of the many-faceted truth of the resurrection of Jesus. And like the diamond, it can be turned this way or that in order to reveal yet another precious aspect. It provides exceptional evidence for Christian Theism. It is linked to many of the most important biblical doctrines, as well. But it also provides the catalyst to live so many daily aspects of the Christian life, radically committed to our Lord and Master. As if all of this is not enough, the resurrection of Jesus guarantees that our resurrec-

The Center of New Testament Theology 115

tion and eternal home in heaven await those who have responded to the Lord in faith!

APPLICATION

Arriving at the conclusion of this little volume, we will note three final points for application. With the background we have given so far, these will be stated with little elaboration.

First, we have much to learn about the resurrection and the central place that it occupies in the New Testament message. The events of the gospel are mentioned so frequently that their significance might be taken for granted at times, even by Christians. We would be rewarded by the careful study of the place of Jesus' resurrection in Scripture. Further, the integration between the resurrection and a host of other doctrines provides an even deeper pool for learning and reflection. What this event reveals about God is priceless by itself.

Second, the encouragement to apply the deepest truths of Christianity to our Christian lives is an equally exciting challenge that is derived from the truth and nature of this event. The resurrection of Jesus and the eternal life of heaven to which it points should inspire Christians to a deep sense of commitment to God. There should be no tendency to revel in the truth of these doctrines without a corresponding interest in practicing their implications. This point is so important that we will devote a second, companion volume to plumbing its depths.

Third, we have seen how the New Testament states that believers don't have to wait until the future in order to experience the first installment of eternal life, for it begins *now* for those who are in Christ Jesus (John 3:36; 6:47; 1 John 5:13). As Paul states, we are already citizens of heaven (Phil. 3:20). We not only need to rejoice in such truth but to drink deeply of its fountain, allowing it to flow into our hearts. God has *already* allowed us to have a foretaste of eternity!

Thus, we should practice the "top-down" heavenly perspective, applying it to all of life. In a biblical sense, we need to seek our Lord and obey Him by laying up heavenly treasures rather than earthly ones. Jesus has indeed risen from the dead, so our obligation is to place God's interests above ours — to develop a new vantage point from which to live.

> We should practice the "top-down" heavenly perspective, applying it to all of life.

We conclude where we started, by stating that the truth of the resurrection is central to the New Testament. In this event, God's revelation reached a crescendo that has never yet been equaled in history. Yet, it is only a foretaste of things to come — eternal blessings are in store for the believer (Eph. 2:1-7).

NOTES

1. In the second volume, *The Resurrection: Heart of the Christian Life*, we will see that this event is also related to the birth of the church, transformed lives, evangelism, and church planting. Further, it is also used in the New Testament to deal with doubting, grieving, and hurting believers, to provide an example of the daily power available to us for conquering sin, and as the reason we should be radically committed to God. It is even the basis for conquering the fear of death. In these practical realms, we will emphasize that studying and applying the truth of the resurrection can definitely change lives.

2. These seven books are 2 Thessalonians, Philemon, James, 2 Peter, 2 John, 3 John, Jude. Four of these texts are only one chapter long and are fairly confined in their scope.

3. Examples include 2 Thess. 2:14; Jas. 2:1; Jude 24-25.

The Center of New Testament Theology

4. Second Thessalonians (1:1; 3:17) and Philemon (vv. 1,9,19) are identified as the works of Paul, while 2 Peter is attributed to Simon Peter (1:1), the author of the first epistle bearing his name. Second and Third John follow in the Johannine corpus that traditionally includes the Gospel and the first epistle of John, as well as Revelation.

5. This appears to be Paul's point in 1 Cor. 9:19-23, where he explains that he is willing to change his method (vv. 19-22a) for the express purpose of leading people to the saving knowledge of Christ (vv. 22b-23). So his approach might vary although the message remains the same. The same theme is found in Acts 13-19, where Paul utilized various approaches in presenting the same gospel message. Sometimes he preached in a straightforward manner (14:7,21). But other times he used evidences of various sorts (14:3,8-10; 17:1-4,31). The method depended on the audience, but the gospel content was not altered.

6. For those who would like to check the data concerning other religions, see especially Norman Anderson, *Christianity and World Religions: The Challenge of Pluralism* (Leicester: Inter-Varsity, 1984); Stephen Neill, *Christian Faith and Other Faiths* (Oxford: Oxford University Press, 1970; Downers Grove, IL: InterVaristy, 1984).

7. For details of an argument like this one, see Habermas, *The Resurrection of Jesus*, Chapters 1-5.

8. For a little more technical application of this alternative approach, see Gary Habermas, "Resurrection Claims in Non-Christian Religions," *Religious Studies*, Vol. 25 (1989), pp. 167-177.

SUGGESTED READINGS

Dobson, C.C. *The Empty Tomb and the Risen Lord.* London: Marshall, Morgan and Scott, n.d. Chapter I.

Ladd, George Eldon. *I Believe in the Resurrection of Jesus.* Grand Rapids: Eerdmans, 1975. Chapter 3.

Reflecting on Lesson Seven

1. Are you convinced that the resurrection of Jesus is the central theme of the New Testament? Can you name other passages or angles that expand the information presented in this book?

2. When we say that the resurrection is related to almost every fundamental doctrine in the New Testament, what beliefs do you think we have in mind? How do we distinguish between fundamental and nonfundamental doctrines? How does Scripture do it? How have Christians traditionally done it?

3. We commented that sometimes we need to zero in on particular truths and meditate deeply on them, rather than take the general approach we have taken in this book. Pick a specific truth that we mentioned and focus on it in detail. What does Scripture teach about it? How is it related to Jesus' resurrection? What gems can you dig out of it?

4. What does the resurrection tell us about God's nature? What other truths regarding Him can you think of besides those mentioned in this chapter?

5. For group discussion: Invent a witnessing situation. How would you relate to a particular "modern" standpoint that involves the resurrection, such as a New Age outlook? What about someone who thinks that the first rule of religion is that we should never say that any one religion is the only true approach to God? What are some of the issues? How would you answer? Provide as many responses as you can

About the Author

Gary R. Habermas received his B.R.E. from William Tyndale College, M.A. from the University of Detroit, D.D. from Emmanuel College, Oxford, England, and Ph.D. from Michigan State University. He has ministered in three churches, the last being the Chicago Avenue United Brethren Church in Kalamazoo, Michigan. He taught Apologetics and Philosophy at Big Sky Bible College and served as Associate Professor of Apologetics and Philosophy of Religion at William Tyndale College. From 1981 to the present he is Professor in the Department of Philosophy and Theology (Chairman since 1988) at Liberty University in Lynchburg, Virginia. Gary is also the Director of the M.A. program in Apologetics.

Gary, his wife, Eileen, and their children live in Lynchburg, Virginia. Gary has been a member of the Virginia Philosophical Association, the Conference on Faith and History, the Evangelical Theological Society, and the Evangelical Philosophical Society as national President, Vice-President, and Secretary-Treasurer. He has written extensively on the subjects of the Resurrection and Christian Evidences, incuding the following books:

Beyond Death: Exploring the Evidence for Immortality (Crossway, 1998).

In Defense of Miracles: A Comprehensive Case for God's Action in History co-edited with Doug Geivett (InterVarsity, 1997).

The Historical Jesus: Ancient Evidence for the Life of Christ (College Press, 1996).

Why Believe? God Exists! Rethinking the Case for God and Christianity with Terry Miethe (College Press, 1993).

Dealing With Doubt (Moody Press, 1990).

Did Jesus Rise from the Dead? The Resurrection Debate with Antony Flew, edited by Terry Miethe (Harper and Row, 1987).

Ancient Evidence for the Life of Jesus: Historical Records of His Death and Resurrection (Thomas Nelson, 1984); retitled, *The Verdict of History: Conclusive Evidence for the Life of Jesus*, 1988.

The Resurrection of Jesus: An Apologetic (Baker, 1980; University Press of America, 1984).

In addition to books on resurrection written from a scholarly viewpoint, he has also written of his own personal encounter with the subject on the death of his first wife in the College Press book *Forever Loved: A Personal Account of Grief and Resurrection*.

www.ingramcontent.com/pod-product-compliance
Lightning Source LLC
Chambersburg PA
CBHW060332050426
42449CB00011B/2734